Praise for *Saying the Wrong Thing*

"This book takes the tools of psychological flexibility and brings them where they're needed most: into conversations that matter. Moyer, Gerber, and Tucker have crafted a compassionate, practical, and deeply human workbook grounded in ACT principles but aimed at everyday life. If you've ever held back from speaking up for fear of saying the wrong thing, this book will help you show up anyway—more centered, more grounded, and more connected to what truly matters."

—**STEVEN C. HAYES, PhD,** foundation professor emeritus of psychology at the University of Nevada, Reno, and originator of acceptance and commitment therapy

"In a world where fear so often keeps us quiet, *Saying the Wrong Thing* is a much-needed invitation to speak up. With compelling case examples and transformational practices, this book offers evidence-based strategies for readers to courageously, compassionately, and effectively use their voices when doing so deeply matters to them. A must-read for anyone who wants to meet hard conversations head-on with openness, integrity, and heart."

—**JILL STODDARD, PhD,** author of *Be Mighty* and *Imposter No More*, coauthor of *The Big Book of ACT Metaphors*, and cohost of the top behavioral science podcast *Psychologists Off the Clock*

"Do you ever hold back because you're afraid of saying the wrong thing? Avoid conflict or feedback? Fight, fly, freeze, or fawn in the heat of a difficult conversation? If so, help is on the way! *Saying the Wrong Thing* gives us the communication skills and psychological flexibility tools we all need to get better at speaking up. Read this book if you want to be more effective and courageous in all kinds of important conversations."

—**DEBBIE SORENSEN, PhD,** clinical psychologist, cohost of the podcast *Psychologists Off the Clock*, author of *ACT for Burnout*, and coauthor of the *ACT Daily Journal*

"*Saying the Wrong Thing* is exactly the kind of book our world needs right now: a guide for having the difficult conversations that move us toward our values even when conflict feels inevitable. The authors' wise yet humble approach combines deep insight with warmth, offering practical wisdom for the conversations that challenge us most. It's the perfect resource I find myself recommending to clients as a complement to our therapeutic work, helping transform avoidance into authentic, values-driven action."

—**JENNA LEJEUNE, PhD,** licensed psychologist, ACT peer-reviewed trainer, and coauthor of *Values in Therapy: A Clinician's Guide to Helping Clients Explore Values, Increase Psychological Flexibility, and Live a More Meaningful Life*

"*Saying the Wrong Thing* is an extremely comprehensive, thoughtful, and practical book. The authors' authenticity and dedication to their own values are obvious in every chapter and particularly inspiring. It's rare to find such a perfect balance between expertise and humility."

—MATTHIEU VILLATTE, PhD, coauthor of *Mastering the Clinical Conversation: Language as Intervention*

"In a fragile and polarized society obsessed with comfort and nonchalance at the cost of genuine connections, *Saying the Wrong Thing* is exactly the workbook we need at this moment. Full of accessible experiential exercises, backed by evidence-based psychological science, as well as relatable and culturally grounded anecdotes, this book gently guides the reader toward necessary confrontation and assertiveness. At its core, *Saying the Wrong Thing* shows us that we can't have true intimacy and mutuality without conflict, and that generative conflict is an act of love, not divisiveness."

—DR. HAN REN, licensed psychologist, speaker, mental health content creator (@dr.han.ren), and author of the forthcoming book *The Hyphenated Life*

"You will be doing yourself and the people around you a huge favor by reading this important book! Drawing on the principles of acceptance and commitment therapy, *Saying the Wrong Thing* doesn't just give you communication tips—it provides a road map for approaching even the most difficult discussions with mindful wisdom, courage, and compassion. The authors skillfully combine evidence-based strategies with real-life stories and practical exercises, making the material both deeply relatable and immediately useful. Whether you're navigating conflict at work, tackling sensitive topics at home, or simply striving to communicate with more authenticity, this book offers you the structured guidance and flexible tools to do so more effectively. More than just a resource, it's a companion for building strong, authentic relationships and for showing up as the best version of yourself, especially when conversations get tough."

—CHRIS FRASER, MSW, coauthor of *Freedom: How Teens Can Use Mindful Compassion to Thrive in a Chaotic World and Grow a Purpose-Driven Life*

"In *Saying the Wrong Thing*, Drs. Moyer, Gerber, and Tucker experientially take readers through the core ACT model as it applies to conversation. Clever and fresh 'play and practice' skills are included along with tried-and-true techniques—all with purposeful ties to valued communication. The authors model willingness to experience discomfort and imperfection in the service of authentic connection. I highly recommend this book if you care about speaking to others about difficult topics. And if you want to learn about giraffecats, this is the book for you!"

—AMY R. MURRELL, PhD, peer-reviewed ACT trainer, ACBS fellow, coauthor of *The Joy of Parenting* and *To Be With Me: A Trauma Healing Book for Parents and Children*, and author of the Becca Epps series

"*Saying the Wrong Thing* is a game-changer for anyone trying to find their own voice in a time when so many meaningful things are at stake. I found the stories deeply relatable and the exercises simple but impactful. It's been exciting to see my practice around tough conversations shift toward openness, care, and intention. I will continue to come back to the resources offered here, and I know I'll find something a little different each time!"

—**EMILY K. SANDOZ, PhD, BCBA,** coauthor of *Living with Your Body and Other Things You Hate: How to Let Go of Your Struggle with Body Image Using Acceptance and Commitment Therapy*

"I know readers will find *Saying The Wrong Thing* to be a structured yet compassionate resource to turn to again and again. The visual guides and worksheet format offer an accessible, understandable path to apply research-backed theories and skills to everyday situations. There is a wealth of information in this book, in a format that is flexible and supportive for a wide range of readers. This is a guide I recommend to my clients wholeheartedly."

—**DR. HELEN HSU,** past president of the Asian American Psychological Association and author of *The Healing Trauma Workbook for Asian Americans*

"What an incredibly rich and practical resource—thoughtful, inspiring, and deeply needed. Clinicians, helping professionals, leaders, and anyone who wants to use their voice with courage and compassion will find wisdom here. Drawing on acceptance and commitment therapy, this workbook guides readers on a journey of self-discovery and interpersonal growth, empowering the kinds of conversations our world needs most."

—**MOLLY DAVIS MOON,** therapist, boundaries guide, and author of *The Great All: A Parable of Hope, New Beginnings, and You*

"*Saying The Wrong Thing* is an essential resource for anyone who wants to find their voice and effectively navigate challenging conversations. This timely and original book guides the reader through new ways of speaking their truth with grace and care, even in the presence of controversial or painful topics. The authors offer clear explanations and illuminating real-world examples that culminate in a comprehensive guide to understanding, practicing, and engaging in life's difficult conversations. In a world where genuine and heavy conversations are all too often avoided, this book offers an antidote and road map through the whats and hows of saying what really matters. It is a beacon of hope pointing toward richer communication and deeper human connection."

—**LAURA SILBERSTEIN-TIRCH, PsyD,** clinical psychologist, trainer and director at the Center for Compassion Focused Therapy, and author of *How to Be Nice to Yourself*

SAYING THE WRONG THING

An Acceptance & Commitment Therapy Workbook

HOW TO SPEAK UP in Difficult, Controversial, or Emotionally Charged Conversations

Danielle N. Moyer, PhD | Monica M. Gerber, PhD | Molly S. Tucker, PhD

SAYING THE WRONG THING

Copyright © 2025 by Danielle N. Moyer, Monica M. Gerber, and Molly S. Tucker

Published by
PESI Publishing, Inc.
3839 White Ave
Eau Claire, WI 54703

Cover and interior design by Emily Dyer
Editing by Jenessa Jackson, PhD

ISBN 9781683738732 (print)
ISBN 9781683738749 (ePUB)
ISBN 9781683738756 (ePDF)

All rights reserved.
Printed in the United States of America.

Contents

List of Contributors ix

Introduction 1

PART 1 | A New Way to Engage with Difficult Conversations 7

Chapter 1: Why Read a Book About Saying the Wrong Thing? 9

Chapter 2: Approaching Difficult Conversations with Psychological Flexibility 17

Chapter 3: Foundational Communication Skills 33

PART 2 | Setting the Stage Before You Engage 55

Chapter 4: Getting Present Before Diving In 57

Chapter 5: Finding Your "Why" 81

Chapter 6: The Unintended Cost of Control 105

PART 3 | Your Road Map for Talking About What Matters 129

Chapter 7: Making Space for What Shows Up 131

Chapter 8: Putting Things into Perspective 147

Chapter 9: Finding Compassion for Yourself and Others 173

Chapter 10: Saying the Wrong Thing with Purpose 195

Conclusion: A Work in Progress 215

Bibliography 217

Acknowledgments 223

About the Authors 225

List of Contributors

DOMINIQUE WHITE, PhD, LP (she/her) is a licensed clinical psychologist who received her doctorate degree from Purdue University. She owns Elevate Psychology and Wellness, a private practice in California specializing in mood disorders, trauma-focused care, and psychotic disorders. As a woman of color, Dominique strives to use her expertise in cognitive behavioral therapies, acceptance and commitment therapy, and trauma-informed care to provide integrated therapy to individuals in marginalized and underserved populations.

MAHMOOD BUTT (he/him) is a start-up advisor and investor with a particular interest in supporting underrepresented founders. He also supports American Muslim artists working to improve their representation in media. He lives in the Pacific Northwest with his wife and daughter.

JESS GUERRIERO, MSW, MA (they/them) is a pediatric social worker at a pediatric gender clinic in a large academic medical center. As a queer, nonbinary social worker, they seek to find new ways to inhabit space as a partner in care for youth and their families and break down historical models of mental health gatekeeping. Jess also serves as an adjunct professor, consultant, and field advisor to a wide variety of behavioral and public health learners.

STEPHANIE CALDAS, PhD (she/her) is a clinical psychologist and faculty member in the Department of Child and Adolescent Psychiatry at NYU Langone, and serves as a consultation/liaison psychologist at Hassenfeld Children's Hospital and NYC Health + Hospitals/Bellevue. In addition to direct clinical work with patients and families, she supervises psychiatry and psychology trainees, teaches undergraduates, and is involved in other programmatic and research projects that aim to improve health equity.

ANNETTE L. CANTU, PhD (she/they) is a clinical psychologist at the Portland Anxiety Clinic in Portland, Oregon. As a sensitive, queer, disabled, Mexican American, first-generation college graduate, Dr. Cantu is dedicated to fostering connection and healing through her work and play. Outside of the clinic, she enjoys gardening, reading, frolicking, and building community with others.

SAYING THE *WRONG* THING

NANCY LEE, MA, LPC, NCC, DipCFT (she/her) is a licensed psychotherapist, counselor educator, and mental health advocate. She works in private practice and higher education. Her research focuses on the role of compassion and cultural humility in counseling and teaching.

Introduction

> "Being alive is about messing up, gloriously."
> —Alok Vaid-Menon

Have you ever worried about saying the wrong thing? Have you ever ruminated over whether something you said was socially acceptable or utterly, hopelessly wrong? Have you ever cringed after hearing someone else say something inappropriate, even if unintentional? We have yet to meet a person whose answers are simply "no."

Whether about politics, religion, social justice, mental health, parenting, or grief, we all face difficult conversations, especially when the topic matters and the stakes feel high. When it comes to discussing the painful, controversial, or confusing parts of life, we often go to great lengths to avoid *saying the wrong thing*. We may keep silent when someone makes a racist comment, change the subject when someone mentions religion, or even make a joke to ease the pain of grief. Unfortunately, avoidance often comes at a cost: increased anxiety, isolation, damaged relationships, and more.

As clinical psychologists, we hear more and more that people are afraid of saying the wrong thing—afraid of hurting someone's feelings or igniting a fire they're unprepared to fight. There are many wonderful books available that address conflict management and effective communication skills, but what we are offering is different. Based on a revolutionary treatment approach called acceptance and commitment therapy (ACT, pronounced "act"), this workbook will teach you the skills you need to courageously show up to conversations that are important to you. We hope this workbook will help you talk about what truly matters, even when the fear of saying the wrong thing tries to stand in your way.

Who Is This Book For?

Can you recall what happened the last time someone at work used a microaggression and you decided not to address it? Or when a family member used hurtful words to describe neurodivergent children and you avoided confronting them? What about a time when someone made a misogynistic comment at a family gathering and you nervously laughed it off?

Throughout our lives, we have met countless people who feel like they're always saying the wrong thing, and others who perpetually shy away from situations in which they might—as authors, we are no exception. This book is intended for all of those people. It is for anyone who wants to show up more authentically when having important conversations, especially those who experience uncomfortable emotions when tough topics come up. Perhaps you're a clinician looking for new strategies to help your clients, or maybe your own therapist recommended this book. Perhaps you want to prepare for one very specific conversation, or you're looking to improve your communication skills and relationships on a more global level. No matter your reasons for picking up this book, rest assured that if there's a topic you'd like help talking about, you're in the right place.

What Is in This Book

Throughout this workbook, you'll find a variety of ACT-based tools to help you effectively engage in important conversations, even when they're hard. In **part 1**, we discuss why it can be so difficult to broach certain topics and then introduce ACT as a framework that can help address this dilemma. We also include foundational, tried-and-true communication skills to keep in mind along the way. In **part 2**, we introduce the ACT skills you need to use *before* you engage with a tough topic, like clarifying your values and preempting barriers that are likely to arise. Finally, in **part 3**, we cover the ACT skills you'll need to use *during* and *after* difficult conversations, such as perspective-taking and compassion for yourself and others.

Although the chapters in parts 2 and 3 cover most of the concepts within the ACT model, they are often overlapping and interconnected. We have arranged the material in this way to scaffold your learning and practice, but each concept can be used flexibly at any point in a challenging conversation. Our final chapter will help you plan for future practice and application, since you can't always predict when a heated discussion will arise! Within each of these chapters, you will find:

- An explanation of the specific ACT skill or skills and how they relate to difficult conversations

Introduction

- Real-world examples from our own lives, contributors, and anonymized clients and workshop participants
- Structured activities to help you practice the techniques as you read
- A summary of the strategies covered

At the end of chapters 2 through 10, you will also find a *Play and Practice* section, which offers real-world suggestions for practicing these skills in your daily life. These include activities you can complete on your own as well as activities you can do with another trusted person (ideally someone also reading the book!). After each *Play and Practice* section, you will find templates to complete the referenced exercises. We've found these concepts really shine when practiced in community, so if you can, find someone you trust to work alongside. Once you've done this, we recommend trying out the skills in an actual conversation in your life. You can choose an important conversation and attempt to infuse it with the skills, or you can choose one day where you make an effort to use the skills throughout your daily conversations.

We suggest you take time between reading each chapter to think about and practice each new concept. It may take some experimenting to find expressions of these techniques that work best for you. Of note: Some of the activities in this workbook invite you to connect with the present moment and with your five senses. We want to acknowledge that people may have limitations or differing abilities to engage certain senses. We encourage you to adapt the activities to best support your abilities and learning goals. Additionally, we invite you to engage with the supplemental materials accessible on this book's website: www.sayingthewrongthing.com.

While many of us have moved toward written forms of communication (texting, email, social media), we have found that truly meaningful dialogue is more attainable when it occurs in a verbal format (in-person conversations, phone calls, or video calls). After all, we all know how easy it is to make assumptions about someone's tone or intent on platforms like social media. Use what means of communication are accessible for you as you make your way through this workbook, while keeping in mind that the skills you'll learn are most effective when used in face-to-face conversations, either in person or with the use of video or audio technology.

Social Progress Lens

An important basis for this book is our view that systemic oppression is active in most countries around the world. Because most of us do not fall into powerful roles of making and changing legal policies, we hope this book contributes to a cultural shift where individuals take responsibility for the world they want to share with one another and co-create. This shift is possible, as we saw with the Black Lives Matter movement in the United States over the course of 2020, in which many individuals and companies scrambled to take a stand against racism. However, after the initial wave of support, many people found they did not have the tools or energy to sustainably engage in progressive action. Many felt burned out and eventually shut down or returned to comfortable old patterns. If you care about social progress in our world, as we do, we hope you can use the content of this workbook to *consistently* show up in the face of social justice concerns in ways that feel true to yourself and your values.

We also encourage you to tune in with your needs and to decide when it is simply not safe for you to engage in certain conversations. We aim for a flexible approach that honors your boundaries and safety above all. In the service of this intention, we will offer additional techniques throughout the workbook that you can use to remain aligned with who you are in moments and spaces when it feels safer to disengage.

It would be foolish for us to claim to have this all figured out. After all, we started talking about "saying the wrong thing" to practice working through our own discomforts and hang-ups! Therefore, to supplement and extend beyond our own perspectives, we've invited additional collaborators to contribute content to this workbook. Our contributors have graciously shared their personal stories and additional exercises, which we have incorporated throughout the remainder of this text. As authors and contributors, we have labeled our own stories in the service of authenticity and shared humanity. The views and examples that we all share throughout this workbook are, admittedly, coming from a particular perspective of social progress and what that means to us and our contributors. You may find that some examples do not align with your own values or perspectives, or perhaps invoke discomfort. If this happens, we encourage you to notice and sit with it, revisiting where your own values may fit into the lessons being covered. After all, one of the major aims of this workbook is to help you practice dancing with discomfort effectively. Moreover, when you get out to practice in the real world, you absolutely will be

Introduction

in conversation with others who do not share your point of view. What better time to get acquainted with that feeling than now?

It may also be helpful as a reader to know that, throughout this book, we are primarily speaking from a United States context and perspective. While we hope this book speaks to a global audience, there may be times that the content is heavily influenced by our cultural experiences. We acknowledge that a large majority of psychological science content is produced from this American context, and we encourage any readers who would like to offer their perspective on using this framework in their country to reach out to us via our website so we can expand and uplift more voices in this larger conversation.

Finally, we invite you to approach this content with compassion for yourself and others, and with openness to what it might enable in your life and relationships. This is not a be-all and end-all approach to difficult conversations. We all have different communication styles influenced by our culture, upbringing, and environmental factors. Some styles work better in certain settings than others. Even as psychologists, we are always learning, growing, and—sometimes—saying the wrong thing. You can't control the world around you, the family you were born into, or how your family history plays out in your life. You can, however, alter your relationship with those variables in ways that matter and feel consistent with who you are. If you're ready to show up to the important conversations in your life with confidence and purpose, we can't wait to embark on that journey alongside you.

PART ONE

A New Way to Engage with Difficult Conversations

CHAPTER 1

Why Read a Book About Saying the Wrong Thing?

> "I don't want to say the wrong thing, which I always do. I think I do better when I sing."
>
> —Ella Fitzgerald

You might be asking yourself: *Why would I want to read a book about saying the wrong thing? That's exactly what I'm trying not to do!* We hear you. Whether setting an interpersonal boundary, asserting yourself at work, or talking about politics, religion, social justice, or the loss of a loved one, most of us have been in situations where we worried about saying something that was offensive or hurtful, or that could make a tense situation worse. Often, when we're afraid to discuss something, it is because we care deeply about the topic, the person in front of us, or both. More on this a little later. But first: We would like to tell you who we are and why we thought of writing a book about saying the wrong thing.

About Us

This book started with three friends and colleagues discussing topics for a workshop presentation in the fall of 2019. At the time, we were all working as clinical psychologists for communities with limited access to appropriate mental health care. Although we worked in very different settings, we noticed a common theme: Many of our clients and colleagues (and frankly, friends and family members) were uncomfortable talking about things like systemic oppression, power dynamics, and implicit bias, which are often underlying causes of strife. Time and time again, we heard concerns like "I might make them feel worse if I ask about their loss," or "If I say the wrong thing, they will think I'm racist," and even "I don't know how they will respond. What if they get mad or yell at me?"

So, we decided to formally practice getting uncomfortable by putting together a workshop about communication, interpersonal relationships, and multiculturalism. We invited workshop participants to lean in to challenging conversations of every ilk using ACT as a guiding framework. (We will explain more about ACT and how it will serve as a road map for this book in chapter 2.) What we found was that *all* of our participants felt the impact of increased divisiveness and communication difficulties when navigating tough conversations. Many participants shared that it was liberating simply to hear that others struggled with the same fear of saying the wrong thing! Participants echoed our own sentiments that using the ACT model helped them balance vulnerability, purpose, and skill-building. They especially lauded the workshop's supportive environment, which allowed them to practice finding their own way toward speaking up. Many requested encore offerings of the workshop to delve more deeply into this content.

Since then, we've continued to do just that by incorporating the principles of ACT into additional experiential workshops, our clinical practices, and our personal lives. In doing so, we've watched our colleagues, clients, and selves grow personally and professionally by showing up more authentically and fostering deeper connections within our relationships. We decided to write this book to provide you with the same opportunity—to offer a chance to build the skills needed to work through discomfort and navigate difficult conversations with greater flexibility and ease.

It feels important to note that as three white, cisgender, educated women, we enjoy an enormous amount of privilege and insulation from the challenges that many people grapple with daily. We've tried to promote inclusivity in the use of our own language and examples, as well as through the contributions of our incredible collaborators, who hail from various backgrounds and bring invaluable wisdom, perspective, and depth to this work. We hope that at least some of the real-life examples shared throughout the book serve as illustrations of what you may have in common with lots of other people. We view this as important communal work that will continue to evolve and become richer as you and others with differing perspectives employ it.

Chapter 1: *Why Read a Book About Saying the Wrong Thing?*

Defining "Saying the Wrong Thing"

We have struggled with how to define "saying the wrong thing" because it means different things to each of us. At the same time, something about it seems universal, which is why the exact phrase surfaces again and again in our work and personal lives. Throughout the course of this book, we will share what it has meant to us, our collaborators, and the individuals we serve, and we encourage you to define what it means to you. Here are some example situations we've heard of that sparked fear of saying something offensive, "wrong," or hurtful:

- Asserting your feelings, needs, and boundaries with friends and family
- Communicating how a partner or friend's behavior negatively impacts you
- Discussing differing political views with friends, family, or strangers
- Speaking up when there is a power difference in the relationship:
  - Communicating to your medical provider that you are frustrated, disagree, or feel unheard
  - Speaking up about needs, wants, or problematic dynamics among colleagues and employers
  - Asserting a differing rationale, thought, or feeling to a professor or teacher
- Using pronouns (whether correcting others or being corrected)
- Navigating "coming out" conversations with friends and family
- Telling a prospective dating partner that you're not interested in a relationship
- Discussing parenting preferences or different values in coparenting
- Discussing the COVID-19 pandemic with someone who has different views
- Agreeing to do something and then changing your mind
- Training other professionals about equity, diversity, and inclusion
- Bringing up identity in therapy when therapist and client do not share the same identity
- Speaking up in a meeting that is typically dominated by a few attendees
- Interviewing an applicant from a different cultural background

SAYING THE *WRONG* THING

Do any of these topics resonate with you? Do any stand out or surprise you? Are there others that come to mind? Give some thought to a few topics or conversations that you find difficult or challenging. You can then use these as reference points when applying the ACT framework in the chapters that follow. As new topics come to mind or become relevant, add them to your list along the way.

Difficult topics or conversations you have had in the past:

1. _____
2. _____
3. _____
4. _____
5. _____

Difficult topics or conversations you are expecting to have in the future:

1. _____
2. _____
3. _____
4. _____
5. _____

Other challenging topics or conversations you would like to practice with:

1. _____
2. _____
3. _____
4. _____
5. _____

Although the specific topics tied to "saying the wrong thing" will vary from person to person, there is a common theme that underlies them all: fear or anxiety that the conversation will end badly. We might be afraid that we'll hurt the other person's feelings, offend them, or make them upset. We might be afraid that we'll say something that makes us

Chapter 1: *Why Read a Book About Saying the Wrong Thing?*

sound stupid or uninformed, or that makes the other person like us less. We might be afraid that we'll cause a greater argument, make a problem worse, or fail to get the point across.

These fears are often exacerbated in relationships we care deeply about or in which there is a marked power differential. This fear often holds us back from speaking out and showing up when we know it really matters, or leaves us ruminating for days and weeks on end after a conversation has ended. In the service of authenticity, our first real-life example is from none other than one of the coauthors of this book—Monica—who has the ironic fear of saying the wrong thing while writing a book called *Saying the Wrong Thing*.

Monica's Story—Defining Saying the Wrong Thing

I have spent hours avoiding writing even the outline of this first chapter. Being authentic and striving for inclusivity and equity is incredibly important to me. I have such a hard time defining "saying the wrong thing" for this book because I am terrified that if I leave out someone's experience or get too broad, I'll be seen as a self-serving, narrow-minded dummy who has no business contributing to this project with my brilliant coauthors. I'm worried I won't bring anything to this project—and that my coauthors would definitely be better off without me!

Wow, how mean is that stream of consciousness?! And the pressure I'm putting on myself has only made it harder for me to put words to digital paper. My lifelong fear of not being "good enough" is blinding me to the valuable strengths and experiences I do have. Several times, I've even picked up my phone and started drafting a message to my coauthors saying I should drop out of the project because I'm contributing nothing of value. But instead—in the spirit of this model I profess works so well—I'm slowly breathing and taking a step back from my judgments to reconnect with why it is important to write this book.

As I do so, I remember that psychological science has the potential to uplift society. I care about social progress and creating a world where authenticity is rewarded. I will work to acknowledge and step back from my judgmental mind, while I keep showing up fully every step of the way.

When I take a step back in this way, I remember that "saying the wrong thing" is different for everyone. I struggle to define it at the risk of excluding any relevant part for others, which points to my values. But if I push through that fear, for me "saying the wrong thing" includes anything that could be perceived as incendiary, minimizing, or hurtful when it really matters. I realize these outcomes in themselves are not always necessarily "bad." Sometimes, productive things come from discomfort. The *judgments* inherent in "wrong" or "bad" are what evoke the anxiety that keeps me from saying anything at all and possibly doing more harm in the end. Our goal for this book is to help readers identify and overcome the ways that this fear blocks *them* from meaningful action, whatever that may be.

Chapter 1: *Why Read a Book About Saying the Wrong Thing?*

Why Is It *So* Hard to Talk About *So* Many Things?

We imagine that like us, you really care about the people in your life. To at least some degree, you probably care about the well-being of humanity at large and the health of our planet. But when we care, we can sometimes get caught up in our emotions and struggle to express ourselves. This is one of the tricky ways the human brain can work against us. When emotions are high, our brains flood with chemicals originally intended to shut down critical thinking so we can focus on survival. Our bodies are literally preparing us to run, fight, freeze, or appease the perceived threat. This is especially the case when we feel backed into a corner, even figuratively, like in conversation. That's why no matter how well-versed we are on a topic, or how central it is to our identity or profession, our survival mechanisms can take over when it feels like the social stakes are high. And when critical thinking shuts down, even temporarily, it can feel impossible to work through the mind-fog and even form simple sentences!

This is not necessarily a bad thing. It is a natural function of the nervous system. When we care deeply about a particular issue and are invested in its outcome, it can lead us to fear the potential loss, hurt, rejection, or harm we might experience if it doesn't go our way, which automatically turns on the body's survival system. That's when our natural inclination to appease others may come in. We might let a sexist comment from a coworker slide or ignore a racist remark a family member makes at a holiday dinner. These moments of inaction—the moments when we fail to speak up—don't happen because we are weak or cowardly, but because our brains say it is safer to avoid possibly saying the wrong thing. Many of us also live in cultures that reward us for avoiding controversy to keep the peace. It can be better to keep quiet when an aunt makes a comment about our life choices if it means preventing a larger family conflict.

Our bodies are wired to keep us safe—to avoid conflict that could be detrimental to our well-being. Add to that the high emotional tension from intergenerational trauma, unhealthy family systems, toxic relationships, political unrest, a global pandemic, or systemic oppression, and it can be downright exhausting—not to mention the wide-ranging effects of technology, which is an increasingly prevalent part of our everyday lives and comes with inherent danger. Not only do we fear backlash and the lasting punishment of our mistakes becoming immortalized online, but virtual anonymity allows for cruelty and trolling that have made it feel even riskier to be our full selves.

SAYING THE *WRONG* THING

If you've had times in recent years when you felt like the world was literally burning around you, you're not alone. We feel it too. And when things feel overwhelming, navigating a conversation with someone who fundamentally disagrees with you as to *why* the world is burning can feel impossible. If you're in a caring profession, you've likely experienced burnout or vicarious trauma during your career, putting a strain on how you operate. We all have limits to what we can carry with us emotionally. It's no wonder almost a quarter of the US population is in need of mental health care (Mental Health America, 2021).

This is not to paint a bleak picture of our existence. You *can* build the skills necessary to effectively communicate with authenticity and humanity, which is something the world needs now more than ever if we hope to see social and environmental progress. As you move through this workbook, you will learn to listen to your intuition to gauge when it is safe to lean into a difficult situation or when it is effective to disengage. This flexible approach allows you to honor your boundaries and safety above all.

Since this can be difficult work that is not always rewarded by society, remember to treat yourself with compassion as you begin this journey. Self-compassion is about acknowledging the suffering inherent in much of your reality and still choosing to treat yourself with kindness. You can be more connected and learn more effectively when you apply less pressure and judgment; we invite you to engage with the content in this way. Approach this workbook with openness and honesty, keeping in mind that *you* get to choose how you engage with the material and can adjust it to your level of comfort at any time. We will expand more on compassionate approaches in chapter 9. Now, let's get started.

CHAPTER 2

Approaching Difficult Conversations with Psychological Flexibility

> "I know nothing in the world that has as much power as a word. Sometimes I write one, and I look at it until it begins to shine."
>
> —Emily Dickinson

Have you ever thought about how incredible human language is? We take thousands of sounds and symbols that have no formal relationship to their meaning and put them together in ways that somehow make sense. We can scribble down a simple symbol with two curved lines that come to a point and somehow convey one of the most complex concepts in human existence: love. We can assemble a piece of furniture on the first (or second) try by looking at a few squiggles on a piece of paper labeled "instructions." And we can feel a rush of positive feelings just because a child makes the simple sound "da-da" for the first time. It really is remarkable!

Of course, there is a downside to this potent tool. With the power of language, we can hurt someone's feelings with a single word. We can easily cause others to feel pain, whether intentionally or (more often) by accident. These days, a single post on social media can impact millions of people in an instant. So, when it comes to having an important conversation with someone about a sensitive topic, it's normal to experience a range of thoughts and feelings. What if you accidentally say the wrong thing and hurt their feelings? What if you say something offensive or make the situation worse? What if you cause irreparable harm to the relationship? This is yet another amazing facet of language: We can invoke real physiological anxiety in response to imagined situations that have not yet occurred and may never occur.

> ### Molly's Story—To Speak or Not To Speak?
>
> My husband is passionate about politics, particularly those impacting human rights and our environment; he dutifully remains informed by consuming vetted news sources and engaging in free and fervent dialogue with people of all backgrounds. I deeply admire this about him and am aligned with most of his philosophies. However, for me, engaging in political discourse, even with my most trusted confidant, immediately incites anxiety that borders on physical illness. When he (or anyone) brings up something happening in the world, I can feel my pulse quickening and my stomach turning in knots; either my mind starts racing with possible responses or my eyes completely glaze over as I placidly smile in amiable withdrawal.
>
> Truthfully, I'm not as informed as my husband is. I feel somewhat ashamed of this. I feel afraid of being perceived negatively for asking honest questions or opposing a point. I don't like being in nonreciprocal conversations, particularly where one person is impassioned and I'm unable or unwilling to participate meaningfully. I've observed that my husband can sometimes judge others harshly, and I do not want to be judged. It makes it hard to engage. It feels risky.
>
> I brought this up to him following what I think we both would describe as a political "rant." I shared that I felt anxious, that he felt unapproachable, and that I wanted to be able to learn and be involved in important discourse with him and others, but it didn't feel like there was room or grace for me to show up authentically. He listened and validated where I was coming from. He shared that my silence in these moments leaves him feeling lonely, frustrated, and disappointed to not be able to share this important part of his life with me. I think we both left the conversation feeling like we understood one another better, but not totally absolved of discomfort.
>
> Since then, we have had considerably more discussions about local and global issues. They still make me anxious. We don't always agree on every point. Though I've tried to get more informed, I will never know every relevant fact or figure. It still feels risky—and that's because it is. We both care about these issues and one another. But, at least in this relationship, sharing my fears has promoted some positive change that emboldens me to stay engaged and to be braver in other spaces moving forward.

Chapter 2: *Approaching Difficult Conversations with Psychological Flexibility*

Take a moment to reflect on something you said recently that may have impacted another person (positively or negatively), or something someone said to you that had an emotional impact. How was the information communicated—for example, was it said verbally, via text message, on a social media post?

_____
_____
_____

What emotions came up for you (or the other person) and how quickly did you notice them? How long did the emotions last? How intensely were you (or the other person) affected?

_____
_____
_____

ACT was created specifically with the perils of human language in mind and can be useful in situations like this! Therapists use ACT to help people with a variety of problems such as anxiety, depression, interpersonal strife, and more. Throughout the rest of this chapter, we'll discuss how the ACT framework can help you more effectively manage those pesky thoughts and feelings that come up during difficult conversations. To begin this process, it is important to understand a foundational principle and objective of ACT: psychological flexibility.

Learning to Be More Flexible

Whether or not you've ever heard the term *psychological flexibility* before now, you have responded to situations with psychological flexibility or inflexibility. So, what exactly is it? Psychological flexibility involves being able to adjust your behaviors as needed in a given situation while remaining true to your personal values (Cherry et al., 2021; Hayes et al., 2006). When you act with psychological flexibility, you behave in ways that move you toward your values even when you're upset or challenged. For example, a person with social anxiety who values friendship and community might choose to go to dinner with a friend despite their fears of potential embarrassment.

SAYING THE *WRONG* THING

No one is always psychologically flexible, and sometimes they're quite the opposite. At the other end of the spectrum is *psychological inflexibility*, which is characterized by ineffective attempts to manage distress or challenges. When you're inflexible, you allow your thoughts or feelings to get in the way of your long-term goals. For example, a person decides not to apply for a job because the thought *I'm not good enough* keeps getting in the way. To be clear, we are not saying that applying for a job or going to dinner with a friend is always the right thing to do. Rather, inflexibility occurs when your thoughts and feelings get in the way of your ability to act purposefully and consistently with your values, whatever those may be.

When it comes to difficult or challenging conversations, the fear of saying the wrong thing is one of many thoughts, sensations, and emotions that may interfere with purposeful action. You might have thoughts such as "I'm not smart enough to be a part of that conversation," "People will start to get annoyed if I bring this up again," or "There's no point in bringing this up, nothing is going to change"—all of which can get in the way of starting a conversation. Or you might get the conversation started, but find that sensations such as muscle tension, sweatiness, or shakiness lead you to change the subject or verbally agree with something that you internally disagree with. And of course, your fears about accidentally saying something perceived as offensive, stupid, harsh, annoying, or wrong can interfere with dialogue as well.

When you succumb to these fears, you can sometimes make things worse! Imagine an employee who avoids talking in meetings out of fear of sounding stupid. They might not share an idea that would have been perceived as innovative by leadership, and they may even come across as disinterested or distracted. Or imagine an adult who doesn't correct a family member's offensive and politically incorrect views because they don't think it will make a difference. The offending family member then continues using disrespectful language because they believe they are in the right.

In both examples, psychological inflexibility is keeping the person stuck and preventing them from acting in accordance with their values. The good news is that psychological flexibility is a skill you can practice to engage in more effective, productive, and meaningful conversations. To do so, you need to understand the six components of psychological flexibility (as well as their counterparts—the six components of psychological inflexibility). These are listed in the following table.

Chapter 2: Approaching Difficult Conversations with Psychological Flexibility

Psychological Flexibility	Psychological Inflexibility
1. **Present-moment awareness:** Connecting with the present moment, also known as mindfulness	1. **Inflexible attention:** Being stuck in the past or imagined future
2. **Consciously held values:** Being clear about what matters to you	2. **Lack of values clarity:** Being unaware or disconnected from what matters to you
3. **Experiential acceptance:** Being willing to experience distressing thoughts and feelings	3. **Experiential avoidance:** Attempting to control, eliminate, or deny distressing thoughts and feelings
4. **Cognitive defusion:** Creating distance between yourself and your thoughts and feelings	4. **Cognitive fusion:** Being stuck on certain thoughts and feelings
5. **Flexible perspective-taking:** Recognizing that you are more than your thoughts and feelings	5. **Inflexible perspective-taking:** Being stuck on certain perceptions of yourself and others
6. **Purposeful action:** Acting in ways that move you closer to your values	6. **Inaction:** Acting in ways that keep you stagnant or draw you away from your values

These components of psychological flexibility are interconnected, which is why they are typically depicted in a hexagon shape, or what is known as the "hexaflex" (with its counterpart, psychological inflexibility, being depicted in an "inflexahex"). The following section will provide a brief overview of these six components of psychological flexibility, which are the primary framework for the remainder of this workbook.

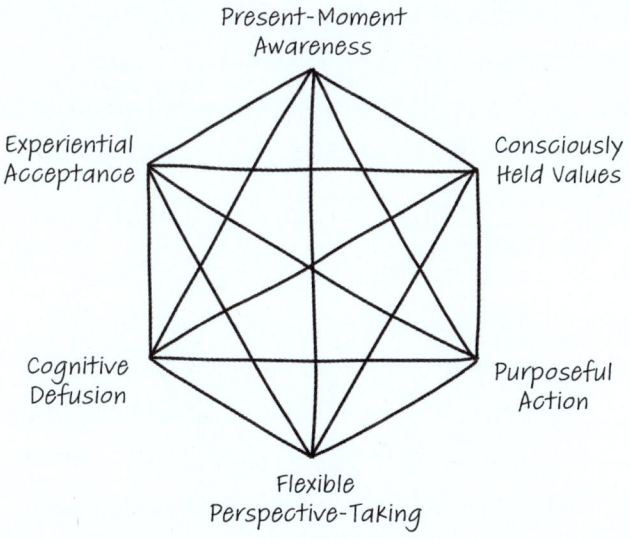

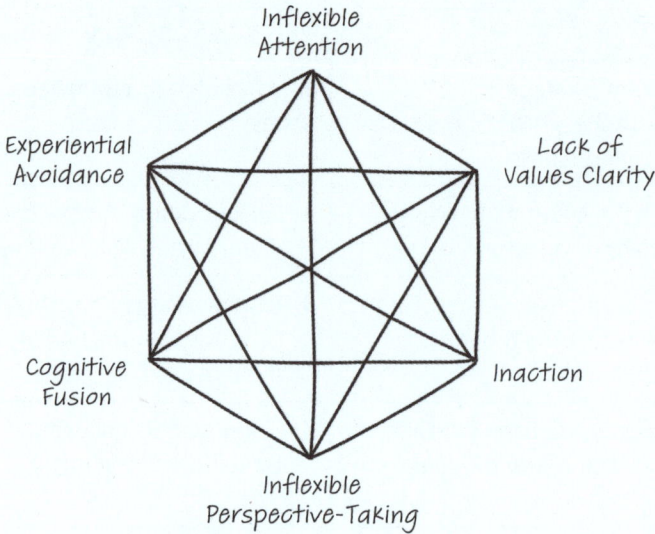

Present-Moment Awareness
(Versus Being Stuck in the Past or Future)

One of the marvels of human language is that it gives us the power to remember the past and to imagine a multiverse of futures that may never occur. The flip side of this amazing ability is that it can sometimes take us out of the present moment. We might ruminate about things that have already happened, overthink what could happen in the future, or dwell on something we wish were different. Psychological inflexibility occurs when we are stuck in an imagined past or future in this way.

Psychological flexibility, in contrast, involves connecting with the present moment and bringing awareness to the here and now. It is about noticing our thoughts, emotions, and sensations as they occur in the moment. This process is also sometimes called mindfulness or mindful awareness. You will learn more about connecting to the present moment (and the consequences of spending too much time in an imagined past or future) in chapter 4.

Consciously Held Values (Versus a Lack of Values Clarity)

The word *value* can have many meanings. Some things have monetary value. Some things might be of value for a particular time or purpose. When we talk about values in the context of psychological flexibility, we are talking about things that bring us *inexhaustible* value. Take health, for example. If health is a value that you hold, there is no endpoint at which the entirety of health can be achieved. It's not a check box on a list, but an ongoing objective that can have several goals related to it along the way. Importantly, the values we

Chapter 2: *Approaching Difficult Conversations with Psychological Flexibility*

are talking about are not imposed on us by others. Our values may be personal, collective, or cultural—and we may (and often do) share values with our family or community—but if a value feels imposed or we have no awareness of its role in our actions, that is different from the values we are talking about in ACT. Whether we freely choose a value or are conscious of a value that has been instilled in us, our values are our own.

On the flip side, psychological inflexibility occurs when we don't have clarity on our own values. We might be unsure about what is important and meaningful to us, or we might feel pressured to act in accordance with values that we do not genuinely align with. At its extreme, this can look like a general lack of purpose or direction, as is often the case in severe depression, or it can simply involve doing activities without consideration of why we are doing them. When these activities are both stressful and devoid of meaning, we may experience feelings of monotony, boredom, or even burnout.

Take a moment to reflect on where you currently stand when it comes to your values. How would you rate yourself on a scale of 0 to 10, where 0 means you have no idea what your values are or can only think of "values" that others have imposed on you, and 10 means you are fully aware of what is important and meaningful to you? You will learn more about identifying and bringing awareness to your values (and the consequences of lacking clarity around values and goals) in chapter 5.

Experiential Acceptance (Versus Avoidance and Control)

When it comes to ACT, it's important to distinguish the word *acceptance* from similar words like *tolerance, approval, excusing,* or *conceding*. Acceptance, in the context of psychological flexibility, does not necessarily mean that we like or approve of an experience. Rather, it means that we acknowledge reality *as it is*, whether or not we like it or agree with it. For example, when a person with a chronic health condition acknowledges the reality of their physical limitations, it can free up mental and emotional energy from an endless battle with the *story* of being a "limited person." Similarly, if the thought *I'm not good enough* is standing in the way of someone's important goals, accepting that thought would not mean that they *agree* with it, but that they work toward their goals *despite* its pesky presence. And when it comes to challenging conversations, acceptance is about being *willing* to talk about topics that are typically anxiety-inducing. You may still feel anxious, but you'll be able to continue anyway with the right tools. *Willingness* is often used interchangeably with *acceptance* to acknowledge the limitations of this term.

In contrast, psychological inflexibility involves attempting to avoid, control, or suppress difficult experiences, which is often ineffective and may even cause more problems. Take the previous examples. A person with a chronic health condition who spends large amounts of energy fighting the reality of their condition may not have any energy left over to give their body the supports it needs. A person who is doing everything they can to avoid the thought *I'm not good enough* may never reach their goals because they are too afraid to risk failure. A person who avoids anxiety-inducing conversations will continue to duck more and more discussions to keep their anxiety at bay. Avoidance may feel like it provides some relief in the moment, but it ultimately leaves you trapped in a cycle of unhelpful behaviors, thoughts, and feelings that keep you separated from what matters. You will learn more about the consequences of avoidance and control strategies in chapter 6 and learn how to build willingness and acceptance skills in chapter 7.

Cognitive Defusion (Versus Being Stuck on Thoughts and Feelings)

In ACT terms, cognitive fusion occurs when you get so stuck on a thought, feeling, or experience that you allow it to completely take over your behavior. Have you ever been hooked on a thought? Perhaps you spent a lot of time ruminating about it, or you became very defensive when someone attempted to tell you otherwise. For example, imagine that you believe that you are a terrible communicator and no one understands what you are truly trying to say. Even if others have given consistent feedback to the contrary, being hooked on, or fused with, this thought of being a bad communicator will likely keep you from speaking up and experiencing any other outcome. In this example, you are exhibiting cognitive fusion, which is a component of psychological inflexibility.

In contrast, cognitive defusion can help you get unstuck by creating healthy distance between yourself and your thoughts, feelings, or experiences. Returning to the previous example, if you take a few steps back from the story of being a bad communicator, you may be able to see all the times you *have* clearly and meaningfully engaged in dialogue or had others express understanding and appreciation for your communication style. When you are able to get a little distance from your thoughts, they have less power to cause distress or interfere with valued actions. You will learn more about defusing from your thoughts (and the consequences of being too stuck on them) in chapter 8.

Chapter 2: *Approaching Difficult Conversations with Psychological Flexibility*

Flexible Perspective-Taking (Versus Being Stuck on Perceptions of Yourself or Others)

There are many different ways that you may view yourself. From your perspective, you may be a parent, a sibling, or a friend. You may base your identity on your profession, your culture, or your relationship status. You may be your best qualities, or you may be your worst qualities. Part of psychological flexibility is being able to see yourself as more than any one of these parts, as a person who transcends any one characteristic, identity, or experience. You are a sum of these—and countless other—parts. And the same is true for others. If you're familiar with ACT, you may have heard terms such as *self-as-context, self-as-process, the observer self,* or *the transcendent self* to describe this component of psychological flexibility. Because all of these terms include aspects of flexible perspective-taking, we use the term *perspective-taking* to refer to this skill.

In contrast, psychological inflexibility involves rigid or underdeveloped perspective-taking skills. Someone with weaker perspective-taking skills will have a harder time seeing things from another point of view or struggle to understand irony or certain humor. Someone with rigid perspective-taking may also over-identify with beliefs about themselves—which can be either negative ("I'm stupid" or "I'm annoying") or positive ("I'm knowledgeable" or "I'm hardworking")—causing them to lose sight of their greater experiences as human beings. Similarly, they may get stuck on singular versions of others, labeling them as "controlling," "uncooperative," "biased," or some other characteristic that lacks nuance. You will learn more about flexible perspective-taking (and the consequences of getting stuck on perceptions of yourself and others) in chapter 8. Additionally, you will also learn how to promote compassion for yourself and others as whole, complicated, and inherently imperfect beings in chapter 9.

Purposeful Actions (Versus Inaction or Mindless Action)

We have chosen to describe this component of psychological flexibility last because, in some ways, it is the summation of all the other skills put together. Once you connect with the present moment, clarify your values, accept whatever comes up in life, defuse from your thoughts, and take a flexible perspective, you have cultivated a space where you can fully choose your actions. When you act with purpose, you are confident that what you do and say is in the service of what matters to you, even if things do not go according to plan. Although this skill is sometimes called *committed action*, we prefer to use the phrase *purposeful action*. This is because many people see the word *commitment* as signifying a one-time decision that you are meant to stick with over the long term—and often assume that there will be no lapses. For example, this is how people tend to regard committed relationships—which can even include official "vows" meant to be followed long term—or twelve-step treatments that require complete abstinence.

With purposeful action, we intend to illustrate that commitment involves making moment-to-moment choices to act consistently with your values, acknowledging this as an ongoing and flexible process that you can adapt. These choices are not automatic but, rather, intentional actions in the present moment. For example, a person with anxiety may say to their therapist, "I wanted to leave the house yesterday, but I couldn't. I failed." However, this person may have taken several values-based, purposeful actions in service of leaving the house, such as getting dressed, texting a friend for accountability, and opening the front door—even if they didn't make it past the front step. A savvy therapist would attempt to turn the client's attention to the purposeful actions they *did* take to help illustrate this process. Even if a larger goal is not necessarily reached, each intentional choice demonstrates psychological flexibility.

Conversely, there are two main ways people tend to exhibit psychological inflexibility in this area: through inaction and mindless action. Let's take these one at a time, starting with inaction.

Look around you and see if there is a pen or other small object close by that you can hold in your hand. Now, *try* to pick it up. Don't actually pick it up! Just *try* to pick it up. Feels strange, doesn't it? This is because we can either act or not act, but there really is no way to do something in between. We often use the word *try* to indicate that an action did not lead to our intended goal, but sometimes we conflate it with an action when it is not. Here are a few examples that illustrate potential inaction: "I tried to speak up in the meeting, but I was too worried about what other people would think." "I was planning to start that new art project, but I didn't have enough motivation." "I wish I had the courage to speak out about this." In each of these situations, energy is directed toward the undesirable—avoiding judgment, struggle, and fear—rather than toward values.

The second way we can be inflexible is via mindless action. You have probably had the experience of driving, walking, or taking some other mode of transit from one place to another and suddenly arriving at your destination with very little recollection of how

Chapter 2: *Approaching Difficult Conversations with Psychological Flexibility*

you got there. This experience of being on autopilot can be a little unnerving! To be clear, we are not suggesting that every action you take must be full of purpose and gumption; that would be unrealistic and exhausting. It is perfectly acceptable to do nothing or relax mindlessly at times. Rather, we are saying that mindless action can contribute to psychological inflexibility when it takes you away from what is important and meaningful to you in the moment. For example, a parent might "zone out" when interacting with their child because they are overly focused on an upcoming work deadline. Conversely, the same parent might struggle to focus on their work because they are ruminating about not spending enough time with their child, which means in the end they give neither activity their full attention. You will learn more about taking purposeful actions (and the consequences of inaction and mindless action) in chapter 10.

These six interconnected skills will serve as a road map as we progress through the remainder of the workbook. In chapters 4 through 10, we will dive deeper into each component of psychological flexibility in the hopes that you can practice it, strengthen it, and then apply it specifically to engaging in difficult conversations. However, we would be remiss if we didn't also review a few tried-and-true skills that lay the foundation for effective communication and productive conflict resolution. These include skills such as active listening, radical candor, and empathy, to name a few, which we will discuss in the next chapter.

SAYING THE *WRONG* THING

Play and Practice

- Go back to each of the six processes of psychological flexibility (and inflexibility) and try to recall examples from your own life that illustrate each point. Write down at least one example for each. You can also use the *My (In)Flexibility Examples* template provided at the end of this chapter. If you're struggling to come up with examples, try first thinking of times you've seen others demonstrate each skill; then see if you can recall anything similar from your own life. Take note of areas that come to mind easily versus effortfully.

- As with all skills, we tend to have areas of psychological flexibility that are personal strengths and other areas with room for improvement. Use the provided *Hexaflex Strengths & Areas of Growth* template to take some notes about your current self-perception. Use a highlighter or a colored pen or pencil to indicate areas that you see as current strengths for yourself. Use a different color to highlight areas that you have more room to grow. Revisit these notes as you progress through the workbook to see whether there are changes, improvements, or skills that take longer than others to hone.

- Take notice of the different aspects of psychological flexibility and inflexibility in film and media conversations. Choose your favorite reality television show (treasure troves of heated conversations!) and try to identify when people are being more or less flexible and how. Pick up a new book (or an old favorite) and take notes in the margins when characters are discussing difficult topics, noting examples of avoidance, clear values, or trouble with perspective-taking. Instead of suffering through ads with nothing better to do than wait for your content to resume, challenge yourself to identify these skills even in quick clips. (Is the man who's enjoying the smell of fresh laundry successfully contacting the present moment? Are the athletes in the ad appealing to any of your shared values? Is it really an exclusive offer, or is the ad capitalizing on people's fear of missing out on things?)

Chapter 2: *Approaching Difficult Conversations with Psychological Flexibility*

> ## Takeaway Points
>
> - Language and cognition are powerful tools, but they can also be the source of pain and suffering. When you let thoughts and feelings get in the way of pursuing what matters to you, this is called psychological inflexibility.
>
> - Psychological flexibility allows you to effectively manage your thoughts and feelings in the service of valued actions. ACT aims to build the six interconnected skills that make up psychological flexibility.
>
> - The six skills of psychological flexibility are (1) connecting with the present moment, (2) being aware of your values, (3) being willing to experience distressing thoughts and feelings, (4) creating distance from your thoughts and feelings, (5) perspective-taking, and (6) taking purposeful actions. These six skills (plus a few extras) will be the guide to this workbook.
>
> - Psychological flexibility can help you engage in important or meaningful conversations when your thoughts and fears are threatening to get in the way.

My (In)Flexibility Examples

Psychological Flexibility	Psychological Inflexibility
Present-moment awareness:	**Inflexible attention:**
Consciously held values:	**Lack of values clarity:**
Experiential acceptance:	**Experiential avoidance:**
Cognitive defusion:	**Cognitive fusion:**
Flexible perspective-taking:	**Inflexible perspective-taking:**
Purposeful action:	**Inaction or mindless action:**

Hexaflex Strengths & Areas of Growth

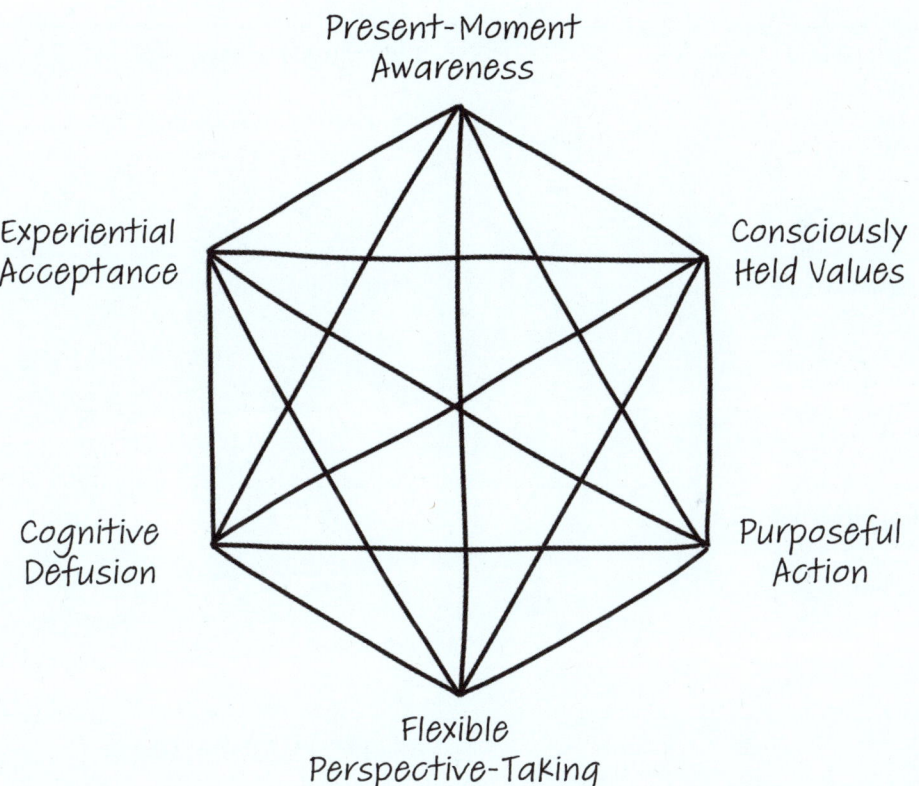

CHAPTER 3

Foundational Communication Skills

> "Not everything that is faced can be changed, but nothing can be changed until it is faced."
> —James Baldwin

While the six components of psychological flexibility are essential to helping you overcome the fear of saying the wrong thing, you also need to learn several foundational communication skills to effectively engage in productive, compassionate, and meaningful conversations. These skills will go a long way in mitigating anxiety and helping you feel more prepared and confident. They are the basics upon which you will build psychological flexibility—even, and especially, in the face of anxiety. The goal is to apply these skills while having conversations in real time. Since it is not possible to master these skills overnight, you need to practice them on a regular basis so you can feel more comfortable and fluid in your application. Although many of these communication skills overlap with the ACT skills you will learn throughout this book, we feel it is important to acknowledge them separately here given their immense value in conflict management and relationship effectiveness.

Active Listening

No book on communication would be complete without mention of active listening. First coined by Carl Rogers and Richard Farson in 1957, the term *active listening* involves three primary components: (1) making an intentional effort to understand the other person by listening for the full meaning of what they are saying, (2) asking for clarification when needed, and (3) reflecting back what you heard them say to ensure you understand. This demonstrates that you care about what the other person is saying, while minimizing the potential for miscommunication. While there are many micro skills that can improve active listening, and a quick internet search will produce a multitude of "top active listening skills" lists, it is really these three components that form the basis of this skill. Let's go through each of these three components in greater detail.

The first component involves **listening for the meaning** behind what someone is saying, as opposed to simply listening to the overt content. For example, a colleague comes to you and says, "I finally finished that big project." If their tone of voice, body language, and facial expression suggest that they are proud, you might respond with congratulations. On the other hand, if their tone of voice, eye roll, and emphasis on the word *finally* suggest that they did not enjoy working on this project, you may respond with sympathy and validate their frustration. The point is, how you chose to respond is based on more than just the content of their words—it's also about the meaning behind them. If you are distracted or more focused on your own needs, you might overlook these subtle cues and miss an opportunity to connect with the other person more deeply.

The second component involves **asking questions** when clarification is needed, rather than making assumptions about what you've heard. Imagine your friend has a history of ending relationships quickly and then regretting it. This friend is asking for advice about their new romantic partner, whom they claim is too stubborn to continue dating. You feel a tinge of frustration and respond by saying, "You said that about the last person, just give this one a chance." This is more likely to make your friend defensive and shut down. Alternatively, you could use active listening to ask clarifying questions: "What are some examples of this person being stubborn?" "Can you tell me more about what you *do* like about them?" and "What are you worried might happen if you continue in this relationship?"

The third component involves **reflecting back** what you heard the other person say and making inferences based on this information. This can involve paraphrasing the content to confirm your understanding or reflecting back what you believe the other person is feeling. For example, let's say you are working with a student who has not finished an assignment in the time frame you both agreed upon. During your discussion, the student lists all the other tasks they are simultaneously working on that prevented them from finishing the assignment. If you jump to conclusions and believe they are just trying to give you excuses, this may lead you to respond ineffectively and damage the relationship.

Chapter 3: *Foundational Communication Skills*

Instead, you could employ active listening skills by asking, "What I'm hearing is that you have a lot on your plate right now and need some more time to complete this assignment—is that correct?" or "It sounds like you're feeling quite overwhelmed right now—is there anything I can do to support you in completing the assignment?"

Can you think of a time when you wish someone had listened to you in a more active way, as described here? What were the signs that they were not engaging in active listening? How did the conversation end, or what was the result?

_____
_____
_____
_____
_____

What could the other person have done differently to show you that they cared? How might the conversation have ended differently, or what might have been the result, if the other person practiced active listening?

_____
_____
_____
_____
_____

Now think of a time when you wish *you* had used more active listening skills. What were the signs that you were not engaging in active listening? How did the conversation end, or what was the result?

_____
_____
_____
_____
_____

SAYING THE WRONG THING

What could you have done differently to show that you cared? How might the conversation have ended differently, or what might have been the result, if you practiced active listening?

_____
_____
_____
_____

Expressing Yourself with Clarity

Part of effective communication involves asserting your needs and desires in a way that is easy to understand. This can include using "I" statements to clearly articulate your thoughts and feelings, especially when you are angry, upset, or frustrated. "I" statements allow you to express your concerns without blaming or criticizing the other person, which minimizes the potential that they'll become defensive or shut down. These statements usually follow this general format:

I feel [*state what you are feeling*] when [*describe the situation*].

In addition to using "I" statements, you can express yourself with greater clarity by practicing what you want to say ahead of time or getting feedback from close friends about whether your message is clear. You want to be concise and get to the main point of your message quickly. The more specific you can be about what you are asking for, the more likely the other person will understand and give a more definitive response. Finally, be mindful of tone and body language, and use these aspects of communication to bolster your message rather than cloud it. Here are some examples of expressing yourself with clarity.

Chapter 3: *Foundational Communication Skills*

Strategy	Instead of...	Try...
Describe your experience using "I" statements.	"You always ignore my opinions."	"I felt hurt and as if my opinion was not important when you changed the subject abruptly."
Prepare ahead of time.	"Obviously you don't understand where I'm coming from, so let's just agree to disagree."	"I feel like I'm not articulating this well. Can we revisit this conversation tomorrow after I've had some time to think about what I'm trying to say?"
Be concise.	"It's possible that I might have lacked a full understanding of the situation, but I also think it's possible that maybe you didn't fully grasp the situation either."	"I think there's been a misunderstanding on both our parts."
Get to the point.	You list all the reasons why you are unable to complete a task and then conclude with "So obviously there's no way I can finish this by the end of the week."	Start with "I need additional time to complete this task. I can have it complete by next week." Only add additional details if asked.
Be specific about what you want or need.	"I work so hard for this company, and no one even cares."	"I would like more recognition for the work I do," or "I want to be considered for promotion based on my performance."
Use nonverbal language effectively.	You have your hands in your pockets and look toward the floor or ceiling to avoid feeling awkward.	Make eye contact and use gestures, as appropriate. If it's an awkward conversation, then awkwardness may be more genuine.

Exercise—Expressing Yourself with Clarity

For practice, come up with your own examples of poor communication based on things you (or other people) have said or done in a conversation. Next, think about what you could change about the content or delivery to more clearly express the intended message. Notice if some strategies are easier or harder for you so that you know which might require more practice ahead of difficult conversations.

SAYING THE *WRONG* THING

Strategy	Instead of...	Try...
Describe your experience using "I" statements.		
Prepare ahead of time.		
Be concise.		
Get to the point.		
Be specific about what you want or need.		
Use nonverbal language effectively.		

Chapter 3: *Foundational Communication Skills*

Empathy

Empathy is a basic, yet critical, interpersonal skill. Put simply, empathy is the ability to both understand *and* care about another person's experience. When you express empathy, you put yourself in another person's shoes and imagine what they might be feeling and thinking in that moment. For example, imagine you are trying to help an upset patron at your job. You are frustrated because this person appears too agitated to hear the helpful information you are trying to provide. Rather than meeting their frustration with equal pushback and possible escalation, you could take an empathic perspective by both understanding *and* caring for the other person's feelings. You could try to better understand their frustration by reflecting on times when you, too, have felt angry, irritated, or helpless.

Empathy is such an important cornerstone of effective communication because it lets the other person know that you hear them and understand where they are coming from. Unfortunately, most of us do not automatically express empathy when someone describes a problem. So often, we are tempted to offer a solution when the other person is simply looking for an empathetic ear. For example, we may try to make the situation about ourselves by describing something similar that happened to us, or even one-up the person with a more difficult situation or problem. Or we may jump into problem-solving mode or minimize the situation in an attempt to make the other person feel better. Here are some examples of how you can express empathy instead of engaging in automatic responses.

Situation	Instead of...	Try...
A friend tells you about a fight they had with their partner.	Making it about you: "Yeah, that sounds just like the fights I used to have with my ex."	"I imagine you're feeling down. Do you want to talk more about it?"
Your coworker complains about having too much work to do.	Problem-solving: "Have you tried this new app? It's great at improving efficiency."	"That sounds hard. Which tasks are causing you the most stress?"
Your boss gives you negative feedback in your performance review.	Assuming negative intent: "He just doesn't want to promote me!"	"I would have a really hard time giving this kind of feedback to someone."

SAYING THE *WRONG* THING

Situation	Instead of...	Try...
Your family member disagrees with your point of view.	Leading with emotions: "You must not even care if you think that way."	"Help me understand where you're coming from."
A colleague comes to you worried about their performance review.	Minimizing: "Don't worry, these don't mean anything. You'll be fine."	"It sounds like you are worried. What do you think will happen?"
Someone working under you admits that they made a mistake.	Focusing on how the situation impacts you: "I guess I'll have to find time to fix the situation."	"Thank you for letting me know. That must have been tough to admit."

After reviewing this list, take a moment to reflect on how you tend to show up to conversations, particularly those when another person is struggling with something, and briefly write about those tendencies here.

_____
_____
_____
_____
_____
_____

Radical Candor

Coined by Kim Scott (2019), radical candor reflects the intersection of empathy and assertiveness. In conversation, this involves being caring and empathetic toward the other person, while also directly challenging them when appropriate. Radical candor has largely been discussed in the context of providing negative feedback, which can be either spontaneous or incorporated into a structured feedback system, as is the case with employee performance reviews or mid-semester student feedback (Mharapara & Staniland, 2020). When you provide feedback that is both honest and empathetic, people are less likely to become defensive and more likely to act on the feedback by making improvements.

Chapter 3: *Foundational Communication Skills*

However, you can probably imagine what often goes wrong when one of the two components of radical candor is missing. If someone is very caring but uncomfortable giving honest feedback, they may simply provide the other person with praise that is unlikely to help them improve in any way. On the other hand, if someone provides honest feedback without much care or empathy, their delivery may come across as too harsh, leading the other person to feel hurt, distanced, or defensive. The following diagram illustrates these less useful alternatives to radical candor.

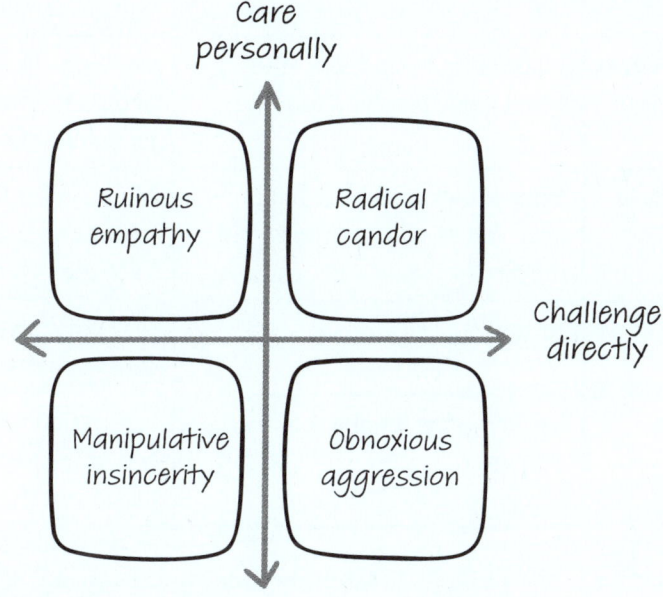

Adapted from Radical Candor: Fully Revised & Updated Edition: Be a Kick-Ass Boss Without Losing Your Humanity *(p. xii), by K. Scott, 2019, St. Martin's Press.*

Other important elements of radical candor include giving feedback in a timely manner, demonstrating humility, and using the appropriate delivery method. When it comes to timeliness, providing immediate feedback allows the recipient the opportunity to make relevant changes in real time. Waiting too long to provide feedback may have a less meaningful impact or may strain the relationship if it feels like information was withheld. In addition, you want to demonstrate humility by being open to information that contradicts your feedback. Remember that your feedback is meant to improve someone's behavior; it's not a judgment of them as a person. Finally, you ideally want to deliver feedback in person, since this best conveys empathy and care. If you cannot give feedback in person, the next best option is to do so via video, followed by at least audio. Written feedback is the least likely to convey an appropriate amount of care or to facilitate dialogue.

SAYING THE *WRONG* THING

Here are some of the potential pitfalls of giving feedback without radical candor, using the simple example of noticing that someone's shirt is inside out.

Pitfall	Feedback Delivery	Potential Results
Obnoxious aggression	Announcing in front of several people that their shirt is inside out	Embarrassment; damaged relationship
Ruinous empathy	Sparing their feelings by not telling them at all	Unable to fix the problem; more people may notice; delayed embarrassment
Manipulative insincerity	Whispering to someone else about it and laughing together	Unable to fix the problem; more people *will* notice; delayed embarrassment; anger
Untimely	Being honest and kind, but only once you've reached the end of the day	More people likely noticed; frustration that they could have fixed their shirt sooner
Indirect	Texting	May not convey the intended care; embarrassment
Arrogant	Assuming the feedback is warranted	Frustration that you assumed it was unintentional (maybe it was inside-out shirt day!)

In contrast to the examples listed in the table, practicing radical candor could involve pulling the person to the side and whispering in a kind voice, "Hey, I just noticed your shirt is inside out and wanted to let you know in case it wasn't on purpose." Perhaps the person will still feel a small amount of embarrassment, but it is likely to be short-lived and overshadowed by appreciation for the opportunity to fix the problem sooner rather than later.

Think of a time when you were given negative feedback in your life. How was the delivery? Did the other person convey both honesty *and* care, or was either component missing?

_____
_____
_____
_____
_____

Chapter 3: *Foundational Communication Skills*

Did you find the feedback to be helpful? Did you believe it to be accurate, or did you feel pulled to argue or contradict the feedback?

_____
_____
_____
_____
_____

How did the delivery impact your relationship? Is there anything the other person could have done to improve their delivery?

_____
_____
_____
_____
_____

Similarly, think of a time when you needed to provide feedback to someone else. This could be formal feedback you provided to an employee, student, or other person as part of work, or it could be informal feedback you provided to a friend, colleague, or family member. What was your motivation for providing the feedback? Were you able to convey both honesty and care? Was one or the other more difficult?

_____
_____
_____
_____
_____

SAYING THE *WRONG* THING

How did the other person react to the feedback? What impact did it have on your relationship? Is there anything you could have done to improve your delivery?

_____
_____
_____
_____
_____

Monica's Story—More Than Simply "Not Having a Filter"

Recently, I decided to provide feedback to my supervisor, who had become increasingly sharp and abrasive during an agency merger. I expected it to be difficult and uncomfortable, but without feedback, my supervisor may not have even realized the impact she was having on the work environment. At the same time, if this feedback wasn't taken well, I worried that things could get worse.

I decided this would be a good time to practice my radical candor skills and approached my supervisor with the following: "I know that you are under an incredible amount of pressure right now, and you are being put in a very difficult position to enact new changes while still upholding our team values and supporting us in these changes. At the same time, I've noticed you on the verge of yelling at several of us over small things, and it feels like it's moved past simply 'not having a filter.' Several people on our team are not comfortable coming to you right now for things that only you can solve. We really need you to take care of yourself right now and ask us to help where we can. You shouldn't have to carry this weight alone, but you also can't take it out on us—we need to feel safe coming to you with problems."

My supervisor shared that she had not realized how her stress was impacting her and her colleagues, and she thanked me for the honest feedback. While the stress continued, my supervisor did start asking for more help and taking better care of herself outside work to manage the pressure.

Although radical candor is perhaps most relevant to the context of feedback, we believe it can be a useful communication tool in any difficult conversation. For example, perhaps there is conflict among your employees, and you need to bring them together to resolve that conflict. You might use radical candor to start the conversation by (1) letting them know that their experiences are important and valid, and that their feelings will be taken seriously, and (2) making it clear that this conflict is interfering with productivity and will need to be resolved. By modeling radical candor, you are setting the tone and modeling for others to do the same.

In your early practice with radical candor, it is helpful to ask the person on the receiving end for feedback on your communication style. Did the other person feel cared for, even while being challenged? Did they understand the point you were making and its significance, even while feeling heard? We know that being authentic in this way can feel vulnerable and even scary, and we are hopeful that the skills you learn throughout this workbook will help you to manage this fear.

Establishing Situational Safety

Finally, we want to take a moment to acknowledge that it is not necessary to engage in all challenging conversations, even when they seem important. The approach we offer in this book is good and well when you want to have conversations with people who hold similar perspectives and values. But what happens when you're faced with people who hold significantly opposing views? Do we still recommend that you take their perspective and embody vulnerability? How much distress should someone be willing to experience, especially when they don't know the potential outcome of the conversation?

We do think there's a line. You should not feel pressured to engage in conversation with people who are actively perpetuating violence against you or your loved ones. But it is your responsibility to find that line for yourself. A transgender child should not have to stand before a judge and courtroom to defend their own existence and rights—but many have in the past few years. People of color should not have to be on the front lines of the fight against police brutality—but every day, many people put themselves in harm's way to advocate for what's right. Sometimes this level of bravery is meaningful and impactful, and other times it is too dangerous, physically, emotionally, or otherwise. Even with our friends and family members, sometimes the situation calls for mindfulness and vulnerability, while other times it calls for silence and self-preservation. There is no one formula that tells you when to speak up and when to walk away, but there are some questions you can ask yourself to help assess safety, both externally and internally, before choosing to engage.

Dominique's Story—Is This a Safe Space?

I distinctly remember the visceral discomfort I experienced when I felt trapped regarding whether to speak up about a social justice issue among my friends. This occurred at the height of the George Floyd riots, when racial equality and systemic oppression were on the forefront of many people's minds. I was out one evening with a group of close friends when someone asked a charged question. It's relevant to mention that the group consisted of five white men, one white woman, and myself: a Black woman. One man tossed out the hypothetical discussion question, "Do we think that the systemic racism that is always being suggested by the Black Lives Matter movement is actually occurring to this extent, or do you guys think maybe it's being blown out of proportion a bit?"

My heart dropped to the bottom of my stomach; I immediately started sweating and averted my gaze from all six heads that had swiveled in my direction. This wasn't a group of individuals who were used to dissenting opinions, and I felt as though I had no support at that table. I remember asking myself, *Is this a safe space? Can I provide an honest response in this moment, without fear of physical or mental retaliation? Will it even matter if I share my perspective and lived experience if they already believe it's all overblown? Can I even articulate anything given how rattled I am?*

I felt like before I could even figure out *what* to say, I had to rapidly assess whether this was a moment I could even speak up safely. I took some deep breaths and reminded myself that these are people I've known and loved for years, good people at heart who truly do not mean harm. But they've lived a very different life from me. I decided to speak up, as it was my sincere hope that additional knowledge and different perspectives would result in a positive learning experience. I was also mad as hell at being put on the spot like that, and at the philosophical framing of a question that is a painful reality for myself and many others.

Though I felt overwhelmed, I led with honesty (and probably a bit of anger) in my response. I said, "I'm feeling incredibly uncomfortable in this moment. I'm the only minority at this table, and you're all staring at me, asking me to basically *prove* to you that racism is real by offering up my own trauma as an example so you can better understand the issue at hand. I experience racism most days, both overtly and through microaggressions. My life is steeped in the consequences of living in a society that spent hundreds of years intentionally disenfranchising people who look like me. It's great that you guys can sit here and act as though this is a debate or a fun discourse, but this is the reality that I live in."

Chapter 3: *Foundational Communication Skills*

> Everyone was shocked into silence, and I mentally berated myself for not being able to just "play along" and for making everyone uncomfortable. There were a few mumbled apologies and a quick subject change for my efforts. In the weeks following the incident, most of my friends reached out to apologize, committing to educating themselves and making it clear the burden of education shouldn't have been placed on me like that. I hope it did some good overall, because I still cannot think about that experience without feeling my heart rate increase a bit.

Dominique's Exercise—Assessing Situational Safety

Before you decide what you want to say and how you want to say it, it is incredibly important to assess the safety of the situation you are in. Not all situations are created equal, and it's important to take note of how you're feeling to determine whether jumping into a potentially difficult conversation is something that will serve you well.

Take a moment to identify a situation that you would like to speak out about, or that you wished you had spoken out about, and briefly describe the scenario here.

_____
_____
_____
_____
_____

Here are some questions to stop and ask yourself to determine whether this situation is one that you really want to engage in:

Who is this person (or who are these people) you are talking to? How well do you know them?

_____
_____
_____
_____
_____

SAYING THE *WRONG* THING

Do you feel physically and emotionally safe in your current setting? Is there anything in your current environment that could cause additional distress?

_____
_____
_____
_____
_____

How does this person (or how do these people) react when uncomfortable or challenged?

_____
_____
_____
_____
_____

What is your "why"? Why do you believe it is important to speak up at this time?

_____
_____
_____
_____
_____

What else is currently going on in your life? Do you have the mental and emotional space to fully engage in a challenging conversation at this time?

_____
_____
_____
_____
_____

Chapter 3: *Foundational Communication Skills*

There may be times when you don't feel safe expressing an opinion, thought, or perspective that differs from those around you. That's okay. While it is important to engage in challenging conversations and speak up for things you truly believe in, your overall safety and well-being are even more important. It can feel disappointing when you don't speak up about something that matters to you, but having compassion for yourself in these moments is crucial.

Play and Practice

- With a trusted person, write the specific communication skills you want to practice on pieces of paper and put them in a hat or other container. (You can also use the provided *Guess the Communication Skill* template.) Each person selects a paper and keeps the skill they have selected to themselves. Choose a difficult conversation to role-play and set a timer for three minutes. When the timer goes off, try to guess the skill the other person was trying to use. If you're having trouble thinking of a trusted person, try asking a colleague, close friend, household member, or classmate.

- Go on a scavenger hunt! To begin, draw two columns on a piece of paper. In the left column, list all the communication skills you learned in this chapter, and leave the right column blank. (You can also use the provided *Communication Scavenger Hunt* template.) Throughout the day, notice when other people are using the skills in conversation; jot down the scenario you witness next to the accompanying skill in the adjacent left column. You can do this challenge on your own and have a reward ready for when you've spotted them all, or you can do it with a partner and race to see who collects all the skills first.

- Write specific communication skills you want to practice on the squares of a blank bingo card. (You can also use the provided *Communication Bingo* template.) After each conversation you have, reflect on your actions and mark off any skills you remember using. Give yourself a reward once you get a BINGO!

- Role-play (with a trusted person) a difficult conversation you are expecting to have. Provide them with a list of foundational communication skills and have them check off the ones they notice throughout the conversation. (You can also use the provided *Communication Role-Play* template.) At the end, if there are unchecked items, reflect on whether you tried to use them and why the other person didn't notice them. Ask the friend for general feedback about how you did and what could be improved.

Takeaway Points

- Foundational communication skills such as active listening, clarity, empathy, and radical candor will best equip you to approach difficult conversations in your life with mindfulness, acceptance, and purpose.

- Active listening involves three components: listening for the full meaning, asking for clarification, and reflecting back what you hear to ensure understanding.

- Expressing yourself with clarity involves using "I" statements, practicing ahead of time, being concise and specific, and using nonverbal language effectively.

- Practicing empathy lets the other person know you hear them, understand where they are coming from, and care about how they feel.

- Radical candor means being caring and empathic while communicating challenging information directly and clearly.

- It is important to assess your emotional and physical safety before engaging in a potentially charged conversation. Choosing not to engage is a valid option!

Guess the Communication Skill

Active listening: Understand the meaning
Active listening: Ask clarifying questions
Active listening: Reflect back the emotion
Clear communication: Use "I" statements
Clear communication: Be concise
Clear communication: Get to the point
Clear communication: Be specific about your needs
Clear communication: Use nonverbal language effectively
Empathy: Express understanding and care
Radical candor: Be honest and empathetic

Communication Scavenger Hunt

Active listening: Making efforts to understand the meaning	
Active listening: Asking clarifying questions	
Active listening: Reflecting back emotions	
Clear communication: Describing accurately using "I" statements	
Clear communication: Being concise	
Clear communication: Getting to the point	
Clear communication: Being specific about needs	
Clear communication: Using nonverbal language effectively	
Empathy: Expressing both understanding and care	
Radical candor: Being both honest and empathetic	

Communication Bingo

You use radical candor	You use an "I" statement to accurately describe your experience	You give feedback to someone in a timely manner	You use empathy and compassion	Someone else uses an "I" statement effectively
You notice a situation in which more empathy was needed	Someone else is specific about what they need in a conversation	You use all three active listening skills in one conversation (go you!)	Someone else communicates concisely and to the point	You notice a conversation that needs more active listening
Someone else shows they understand the meaning of what you've said	You use nonverbal language effectively	You confirm situational safety	Someone else uses nonverbal communication effectively	You notice someone using radical candor
You are specific about what you need in a conversation	You reflect back someone's emotions	You notice a situation where radical candor may have been a better approach	Someone appears to be empathizing with another person	You deliver information concisely and to the point
Someone asks you a clarifying question to better understand you	You try to understand the true meaning of what's being said	You communicate in person instead of in writing	You ask a clarifying question to better understand someone	Someone reflects back your emotions

Copyright © 2025 Danielle N. Moyer, Monica M. Gerber, and Molly S. Tucker, *Saying the Wrong Thing*. All rights reserved.

Communication Role-Play

Briefly describe the scenario to role-play. Who will you be speaking with? What is the issue you are discussing?

Person: _____

Situation/issue: _____
_____

Check the skills you used:
- ☐ *Active listening:* Made an effort to understand the meaning
- ☐ *Active listening:* Asked clarifying questions
- ☐ *Active listening:* Reflected back emotions
- ☐ *Clear communication:* Described accurately using "I" statements
- ☐ *Clear communication:* Was concise
- ☐ *Clear communication:* Got to the point
- ☐ *Clear communication:* Was specific about needs
- ☐ *Clear communication:* Used nonverbal language effectively
- ☐ *Empathy:* Expressed both understanding and care
- ☐ *Radical candor:* Was both honest and empathetic

General feedback and nonjudgmental observations:
_____
_____
_____
_____
_____
_____
_____
_____

PART TWO

Setting the Stage Before You Engage

CHAPTER 4

Getting Present Before Diving In

> "How we pay attention to the present moment largely determines the character of our experience, and therefore, the quality of our lives."
> —Sam Harris

Take a moment to briefly answer the following questions. You can write down the answers or just think about them.

What was the last thing you ate?
_____

Where were you on your last birthday?
_____

What kind of clothes did you like to wear as a teenager?
_____
_____

Who is the next person you are likely to talk to?
_____
_____

SAYING THE *WRONG* THING

What are you looking forward to in the coming days?

_____
_____
_____

What could be different about your life in a year?

_____
_____
_____

Was that exercise easy or difficult? How quickly did you answer the questions? Was there a question you couldn't answer? Even if you weren't too sure of your answers, we're guessing your mind came up with some things—and relatively quickly. And what's remarkable is that none of these things are happening to you right now! Let's try another set of questions to practice returning your attention to the present (feel free to set the workbook down between questions).

What are three things you can hear or see right now?

_____
_____
_____

What are two things you can physically feel right now?

_____
_____

What is one thing you can smell or taste in this moment?

_____

What is your physical position or posture like?

_____
_____
_____

Chapter 4: *Getting Present Before Diving In*

How is your body moving as you breathe in and out?

_____

_____

_____

How did that feel compared to answering the previous questions about the past and future? Was it any slower or less automatic? Did it come naturally to you, or did it take effort?

One of the greatest challenges of human existence is to simply *Be. Here. Now*—a sentiment explored by yogi and meditation teacher Ram Dass in his 1978 book of the same name. We often find ourselves replaying past mistakes in detail, longing for things to be different or wishing to go back to the way things were. Alternatively, we may find ourselves catapulting into the future, agonizing about possible outcomes and planning for contingencies that may never occur. Unfortunately, preoccupying ourselves with the past and ruminating about the future can cause sadness and anxiety that prevent us from connecting with the beauty and nuance of the present moment.

For example, let's say you are at a family gathering, surrounded by loved ones and celebrating a joyous moment. In this situation, your experience will be determined largely by where your mind is:

- If you are preoccupied with the past, you'll overly engage with memories about other "better" celebrations and wish that this one were different. You may get hung up on the absence of a loved one. You may vividly remember a time when you felt very embarrassed in front of this group of people, or a similar group. As a result, you may be unable to enjoy what is actually happening in the present moment. Indeed, depression tends to find people who are mired in the past.

- If you are ruminating about the future, you may spend the entire party worried about what you will say if you are approached by each guest: *What will I talk about? Will they think I'm weird? What if they get upset? How will I respond if someone brings up X, Y, or Z topic?* You might be concerned about the impression you are making and how it will impact future interactions, many of which will never occur. People who get caught up in the future often find themselves anxious, trapped in their own minds and unable to experience joy in the present.

- If you are mindfully present, you'll be able to attend the party and acknowledge any past experiences or future concerns, but not at the expense of what is happening here and now. You can take in and relish the people, sights, sounds, and smells—and experience the party for what it is. Though many things could happen (or go wrong!), you can choose not to get tied up in imagined possibilities, trusting that you will handle whatever may come (if it ever does at all). You can engage with others authentically and with curiosity, rather than in a controlled or stifled manner.

Becoming stuck in a remembered past or an imagined future is an example of psychological inflexibility or an inability to interact with reality as it is. In this chapter, we introduce the practice of flexibly connecting to the present moment using mindfulness.

Dominique's Story—Bad Therapist

As both a perfectionist and an individual who prides herself on inclusivity and tolerance, I find working with clients from different cultural backgrounds can be daunting. I used to convince myself that I needed to know absolutely everything about a client's culture or religion prior to beginning work with them. As you might imagine, this is *impossible* to accomplish. In doing so, I would set unrealistic expectations for myself and would inadvertently diminish my client's capacity to be open to and accepting of someone who wasn't an expert in all things. This happened during graduate school, when I began working with a young client who was Muslim.

The client indicated on their intake interview that religion didn't play a role in their life or current challenges, so I assumed a working knowledge of the Muslim faith would suffice. But as we began the session, it became apparent that their Islamic faith was so deeply ingrained in how they perceived themselves that it hadn't seemed relevant to acknowledge it separately on the questionnaire. Unable to lean on my typical approach of researching prior to meeting with the client, I felt pure internal panic—impostor syndrome was setting in. My mind dragged me into the quagmire of future-oriented what-ifs, casting judgments on everything I "should" have done. I berated myself for being underprepared, selfish, and a sham: *I should have done more prep work.* My hands felt clammy and my heart began to race as my thoughts spiraled further: *I can't help this person. I'm a fraud. I'm not qualified. This client won't take me seriously. I'm going to somehow deeply offend this person. I'm not a good fit.* My body was still sitting in the room with my client, but my mind wasn't present at all.

I took a deep and (somewhat) calming breath and recognized there was absolutely nothing I could do in this moment to change my level of preparation. I was already

Chapter 4: *Getting Present Before Diving In*

> in it. I knew logically that labeling myself as a "bad therapist" or assuming my client wouldn't want to continue working with me wasn't helping the situation, but it can be so hard to stay rational when you're caught off guard. After a few more deep breaths, I mindfully grounded myself in the present moment. I labeled the emotion I was feeling (nervousness) and decided that what I was feeling didn't have to be good or bad—it could just *be*. Being nervous didn't have to dictate the rest of my actions in session. I considered two paths I could take. Path one would require me to "fake it till I made it," just playing along as though I understood the religious concepts my client was discussing. However, this would render me unable to offer any thoughtful content in response to my client's concerns, a wasteful use of session time.
>
> Path two was scarier. I would have to admit to my client that I wasn't an expert in working with their religion (which ended up being central to the mental health difficulties they were experiencing), but continue that if they were open to my asking questions about their faith and what it meant to them, I would still like to try to work with them. I couldn't imagine knowingly wasting my client's time because I was feeling insecure. I value respect for others too much for that.
>
> Another deep breath in and out . . . and I went with path two. In this instance, owning up to my own limitations in a professional setting and voicing my fears worked out in my favor. My client was incredibly understanding and open to working with me on my knowledge about their religion. We ended up working closely together for months after that. Had I not paused to mindfully reconnect with the present moment, I may have continued forward on autopilot and selected path one, as it required far less vulnerability on my part. While that may have been easier, and certainly less nerve-racking, I feel the path I selected allowed me to honor my own values and meet the needs of my client.

Can you think of a time when you were removed from the present moment during an uncomfortable situation? What was it like? Where was your mind? How did it affect your experience?

_____

_____

_____

_____

_____

Now, reflect on a time when you felt very present in the moment during a time of discomfort. What did you notice? How did you feel?

_____
_____
_____
_____

What Is Mindfulness?

Mindfulness involves intentionally bringing awareness to internal events (e.g., thoughts, emotions, physical sensations) and external events (e.g., sights, sounds, smells in your environment) *without judgment* (Kabat-Zinn, 2003). It is based on the premise that all events are impermanent. That is, experiences come . . . and then they go. Nothing remains constant and everything is changing. When you can recognize and accept this concept in your life, it allows you to interact with your experiences more flexibly. You become less afraid that any feeling will last forever. You are less likely to cling to desired outcomes, knowing that they are impermanent. You can observe any emotion, even an unpleasant one, as it is, understanding its role and function in your life and trusting that you can welcome it like a guest in your home.

There is a common misconception that doing mindfulness "right" (that's a judgment!) will result in a blank, Zen-like state of bliss. This is not so, nor is it the goal. Mindfulness means being aware of what is happening in the present moment—and often, that means being aware of what is *not* blissful, calm, or wanted. For example, with mindfulness, you might find that you're distracted or upset. Or maybe you notice that you are irritable or sad. All of this is normal and okay. All is welcome. In mindfulness, you practice noticing what is there and allowing it to be there, without becoming overly attached. Even the most experienced mindfulness practitioners have days where their minds are uncooperative and emotions are running high. With mindfulness, you learn to remain anchored throughout both stormy weather and calm seas.

Of note, mindfulness itself is a temporary state of mind, not something that can be sustained at all times. With mindfulness, you are choosing to pay attention *on purpose*. In fact, noticing when your mind has wandered and then redirecting it *is* the practice of mindfulness!

Chapter 4: *Getting Present Before Diving In*

Why We Practice

Mindfulness is a skill that requires regular practice. Like any muscle, it will atrophy with disuse. But when you are already busy and overwhelmed, why would you add yet another task to your daily regimen? Well, it turns out there are a lot of reasons! First, mindfulness allows you to create a healthy distance from your thoughts and feelings so you don't become defined or overwhelmed by them. This is crucial when it comes to enacting your values, as mindfulness allows you to see and understand your emotions *beforehand*. Cultivating mindfulness allows you to make values-consistent decisions regardless of the current emotional landscape.

Second, the benefits of mindfulness are well-documented in scientific studies demonstrating that changes in neural pathways occur as a result of regular practice. That's right, mindfulness actually changes your brain functioning! Here are just some of the incredible benefits of engaging in a regular mindfulness practice, if you would like to learn more:

- Greater attention and concentration (Verhaeghen, 2021)
- Improved ability to cope with difficult emotions (Hoge et al., 2021)
- Buffered reactions to acute stress (Morton et al., 2020)
- Reduced work-related burnout (Selič-Zupančič et al., 2023)
- More compassion for self and others (Cheang et al., 2019)
- Deeper connection to others (Winter et al., 2021)
- Reduced depression, anxiety, and stress (Khoury et al., 2013)
- Improved immune function (Dunn & Dimolareva, 2022) and physical health (Howarth et al., 2019)

How We Practice

As mentioned earlier, a crucial component of mindfulness is nonjudgment: It is about experiencing any sensation in the moment with acceptance, nonattachment, and even kind warmth. You can recognize judgment anytime you see extreme language: "good" or "bad," "right" or "wrong," "should" or "shouldn't." These labels tend to be associated with high emotionality and make it challenging to respond with an open mind.

SAYING THE *WRONG* THING

For example, when you experience pain in your body, you might label it as "bad," "intolerable," or "excruciating." Once you become attached to this judgment, you may notice other sensations or emotions that accompany it, like tension, anxiety, anger, sadness, or hopelessness, as well as thoughts like *I can't do anything while I'm feeling this way* or *No one understands what I'm going through*. Those emotions and sensations turn ordinary pain into *suffering* and can lead to unhelpful behaviors, such as giving up, stagnancy, and under- or overexertion. By responding to pain with nonjudgment, you can recognize and respect the pain but remain "zoomed out" enough to see that there are many other experiences happening in any given moment as well. With that comes a choice in how you want to respond. That sense of agency is what differentiates someone who feels self-assured, open, and at peace during hard times from someone who feels angry, victimized, and powerless.

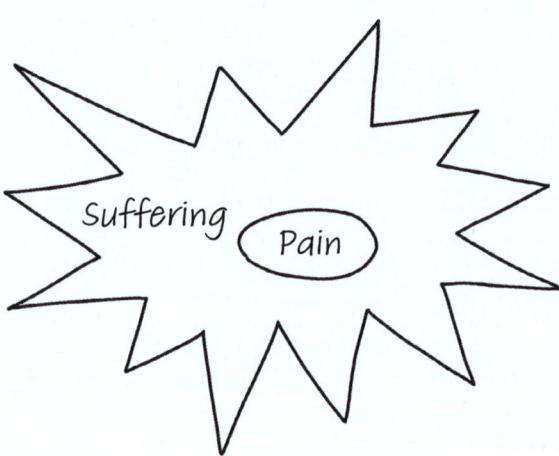

Since observing and describing your experience requires knowing the difference between a physical sensation, an emotion, and a thought, let's take a moment to highlight these three types of experiences:

- **Physical sensations:** These are the feelings you experience in your body: pain, tension, ease, discomfort, temperature, pressure, and so on. Take a moment right now to reflect on what you notice in your body as you read this chapter.

_____
_____
_____
_____

Chapter 4: *Getting Present Before Diving In*

- **Emotions:** Emotions are the automatic reactions you have in response to situations. People often confuse emotions with thoughts—for example, "I feel like you're judging me"—but in this example, the emotion is "embarrassed" or "defensive" and the associated thought is "You're judging me." Here is a feelings wheel to help you identify the different emotions you might experience as you complete the exercises throughout this book:

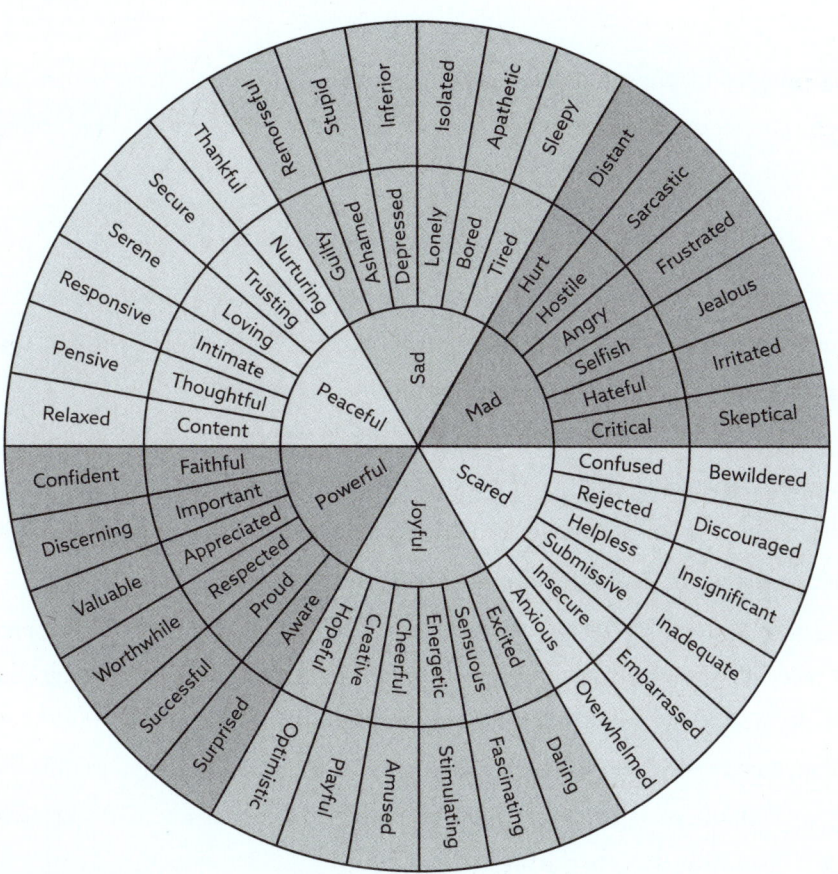

What emotions have you noticed surfacing as you read this chapter?

_____
_____
_____
_____

- **Thoughts:** Thoughts are the opinions, beliefs, or ideas that your mind tells you about why things are happening. When you have a thought, it's like a narrator in your head is telling a story behind each experience. What thoughts are coming up for you as you learn about mindfulness?

_____
_____
_____
_____

Learning about the tenets of mindfulness certainly is useful, but it is best understood through experiential practice. In other words, let's try it with the next three exercises.

Exercise—Mindfulness of Breath

For this practice, you may read along, pausing for several moments between each paragraph, or follow along using this link so you can fully engage without distraction: www.sayingthewrongthing.com/audio/mindfulness-of-breath.

To begin, find a comfortable position, whether it is sitting, standing, or lying down. If you're willing, please close your eyes to minimize distraction, or fix your gaze softly on a place just in front of you. Imagine that your shoulders are relaxing but that a string attached to the top of your head is pulling you gently upright.

Begin by taking some deep breaths at your own pace, perhaps the deepest breaths that you've taken all day. Breathing deeply in through the nose . . . and out through the mouth. As you do, notice any sounds around you: the hum of the air conditioner, the tweet of birds chirping, the whisper of people talking, or even more disruptive sounds like a baby crying, a car alarm, or a power tool. Approach and label each sound with curiosity . . . and then let it go as you return to the breath.

Turning your attention inward, become aware of your body: your feet planted upon the earth, the rise and fall of your chest and abdomen with each inhale and exhale. Briefly scan your body to notice how you're feeling. Maybe there are areas that don't feel comfortable. Send your breath there and allow that to be the case. Now notice areas that feel strong and capable or even neutral. Send your breath there as well.

If your mind is wandering, that's perfectly normal. Each time you notice this and then return to the present moment, *that* is the practice of mindfulness. It may happen many times. Kindly escort your attention back to the breath each time, like you would an excitable puppy.

Chapter 4: *Getting Present Before Diving In*

Now take a moment to consider what made you choose this workbook. Why are you taking the time out of your busy life to learn about engaging in difficult conversations? Notice what comes to mind . . . Images? Memories? Emotions?

As you return to your breath, take a moment to observe how you feel right now. How is it different from when you started the practice? Notice your body. Your thoughts. Your emotions. And take a moment to set an intention for how you might wish to carry this mindful awareness with you as you move throughout the rest of the day. When you're ready, allow your eyes to gently open as you return to this space.

What did you notice from this practice?

General observations:

_____
_____
_____

Physical sensations:

_____
_____
_____

Emotions:

_____
_____
_____

Thoughts:

_____
_____
_____

Breathwork is a foundational mindfulness practice that you can revisit at any time to redirect yourself to the present moment—not just in relationship to having difficult conversations.

SAYING THE WRONG THING

Exercise—Grounding with the Five Senses

Another quick way to get connected with the present moment is to use grounding techniques. One common strategy is to dedicate five minutes (or more!) to being fully present with your five senses. Let's try it. Once again, you may read along, pausing for several moments between each paragraph, or follow along using this link so you can fully engage without distraction: www.sayingthewrongthing.com/audio/five-senses. Feel free to creatively adapt each section of the meditation to fit your unique access to each sense.

To begin, find a comfortable position with your eyes open, and take several deep, cleansing breaths at your own pace. No need to change or force your breath in any way. Just let it flow in and out comfortably.

As you breathe, take a moment to notice your surroundings or anything within your visual field. What do you see? Observe details and nuances that you may never have noticed, even if you've seen this space hundreds of times before. Take in your visual surroundings as though you're a child seeing these things for the very first time. Notice what happens for you physically and emotionally as you do so.

Next, if you are able, become aware of what you hear. These may be obvious sounds, like traffic, voices, or construction; ambient sounds, like an air conditioner; or even things you might not usually notice, like total silence or a slight ringing or buzzing. Observe each sound without judgment, as if it is part of a strange and beautiful symphony that's playing just for you and will never be repeated in this way again.

Now, direct your attention to the sensation of touch. You can reach out with your hands to feel objects in front of you, perhaps briefly closing your eyes so you can notice the contours, textures, and temperature of each item. You might become aware of places where your body is touching your clothing, the ground, or the seat you're on. Perhaps you notice differences in pressure. Get curious about areas you've never considered: How do the backs of your knees feel? Or the tops of your hands?

Next, shift your attention to your sense of smell. Are there any aromas present in the space you're in? Paint, grass, moisture, dust? See how nuanced your perception can be. Can you remove judgment from various smells, appraising things as neither good nor bad, but instead simply as "interesting"?

Finally, what do you taste in this moment? This sense is strongly influenced by smell. How does that affect you right now? Can you taste your toothpaste, your last meal, your own "you-ness"? Again, see if you can remove judgment as you get curious. If you have

Chapter 4: Getting Present Before Diving In

access to something edible, you can take a smell and then a bite, savoring all the changes and sensations that come with even the most commonplace experience.

When you're ready, you can return to your breath and release your attention from this sensory exercise.

What was it like to spend time with your five senses like this?
_____
_____
_____
_____
_____

Exercise—Square Breathing

This next grounding exercise involves syncing your breath to the shape of a square. For this exercise, you may read or follow along using this link so you can fully engage without distraction: www.sayingthewrongthing.com/audio/square-breathing. To begin, find a comfortable position and allow your breath to flow naturally and rhythmically. Then, begin breathing in a slow, specific pattern: inhaling for a count of four, holding the breath for a count of four, exhaling for a count of four, and holding no air for a count of four. Allow yourself a few rounds to find a cadence that works for you. You can visualize the breath moving in the shape of a square, with each edge representing a count of four, as pictured here.

Continue for as long as you wish. Some people find that variations on square breathing work best for them. For example, triangle breathing removes the part where no breath is held, and rectangle breathing involves longer inhales and exhales, with shorter periods of holding breath or no breath. Try a few out and see what works best for you.

Grounding with the Five Senses and *Square Breathing* can be particularly helpful because they are simple, easy to remember, and don't require anything other than yourself. They can be used in most contexts,

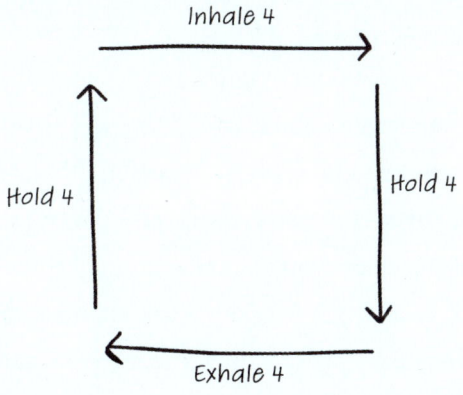

and no one will even know you are using them! If these two exercises don't work for you, there are plenty of others that you can find online. You can also consider mindfulness apps, such as Headspace and Calm, which contain a variety of guided meditations and mindfulness exercises you can choose from. Find a go-to technique that works for you, and you'll always have a way to connect with the present moment when needed.

What Does This Have to Do with Saying the Wrong Thing?

Now that you understand what mindfulness is and have done a little practice, you may still be wondering: What does this have to do with having difficult conversations? A lot. Often, when we would like to speak up but emotions are running high, it is difficult to respond in a way that feels good. How many times have you left an interaction thinking, *Why did I say that?! So stupid!* or *Wow, I can't believe I didn't say anything.* You don't even have to be caught off guard by a conversation for this to happen. You might *know* that you are entering into a difficult conversation with an employer, family member, or friend and be preemptively nervous that you will say the wrong thing (or not say what you wanted to at all). In the following section, we discuss how you can use mindfulness strategies in both scenarios: when you're blindsided by a conversation and when you want to plan for a future conversation.

When You're Blindsided by a Conversation

It is common for challenging conversations to occur suddenly and without warning, or with vague warning, such as the dreaded "Can we talk?" text message. This is sometimes why people choose not to answer a phone call, preferring a text message or email that will allow ample time for planning the "correct" response. Without time to prepare or reflect on your opinions or goals for the conversation, you might be left with little to contribute or uncertainty about how to engage. It would be easy to get distracted by the thoughts, emotions, and physical sensations that come up. In a situation like this, you might experience sweatiness or increased heart rate; you might feel angry, overwhelmed, or even offended; and you might have thoughts such as *Why would they bring this up now?* or *I can't believe what I'm hearing!* If you let these experiences consume you, you're more likely to wind up saying something you regret or, alternatively, nothing at all.

Chapter 4: Getting Present Before Diving In

Molly's Story—Caught Off Guard

My relationship with my father is complex, as many child-parent dynamics are. He is at once someone I greatly admire, someone I'm constantly worried about and trying to help (whether he asks for help or not), and a source of uniquely poignant frustration when we push one another's buttons.

During a phone call some time ago, he asked about my day, and I relayed the highlights. We exchanged stories, and he elaborated on how his experiences might relate to what I was going through. *This is nice!* I thought. I asked how he was doing, and he began to share the stressors of his daily life: difficulties navigating the medical system, an irresponsible landlord and neighbors, house problems, judgmental commentary on family dynamics, and so on.

Overwhelmed by what seemed like a barrage of negativity and immediate problems to be solved, I became tense, my mind involuntarily conducting triage to ascertain where to intervene. *He's unhappy*, I concluded, *and needs my help.* I decided that the medical concerns were the most worrisome and inquired about his doctor's appointments. As my father explained his resistance to the doctor's recommendations, I felt upset by what I perceived to be negligence in his own care, and he felt as though I was being closed-minded. We began arguing about his approach, ultimately becoming too frustrated to continue the conversation effectively and respectfully.

We both ended the phone call angry, hurt, and feeling unheard. Moreover, I felt guilty for being angry because I want to treat my father respectfully, even when we disagree and particularly around decisions that he has a right to make for himself. How he responds or doesn't respond in his own health care is his choice alone, *and* it is scary to stand by and watch someone you love pursue or ignore a course of action that seems likely to prolong their suffering. This dynamic between us is not new—yet, somehow, I feel caught off guard every time.

In situations like this, when you're not anticipating conflict but find yourself poised for a fight, you can use mindfulness to engage with more intention. You can bring yourself fully into the moment to consider how you'd like to contribute meaningfully, even in the presence of difficult thoughts and feelings. To be clear, we do not mean that you can block those experiences or rid yourself of them completely. What you *can* do is notice those pesky thoughts, feelings, and sensations; briefly acknowledge them when they occur; and choose your response accordingly. For easier recall, just remember to *notice and communicate*.

For example, in Molly's situation with her father, these are the elements that she could have taken the time to **notice**:

- **Noticing the body:** "My shoulders have tensed. My heart is beating faster and my breath has followed suit. I'm pacing the room."
- **Noticing the emotions:** "I feel irritated, indignant, and righteous. Underneath, I love and care for him and am afraid for his well-being."
- **Noticing the thoughts:** Attached to the frustrated emotions: "Here we go again," "You *always* do this," and "You're being so *stubborn*!" Attached to the worry: "If you don't treat these ailments, you could die." Attached to love: "I care about you and don't want anything bad to happen."

Noticing your internal experience gives you an opportunity to respond carefully. Once you acknowledge what is happening internally, take a breath and gently shift your attention to the present situation. The next step is to **communicate** with intention; *what* you communicate will vary depending on the person and situation. For example, it is often useful to convey your internal experience. You might say, "I'm noticing that this topic has brought up a lot of emotions for me. Are you feeling that way also?" Or you might request what you need: "I think we should take a break from this conversation and revisit it when we're both calm." Pausing might also give you the clarity to communicate what is actually important to you: "Look, I don't want to argue with you about this. I am just worried about you and want you to be happy." If your internal experiences are warning signs that the context is not a safe one for discussion, you might decide to disengage. This might sound like: "This conversation doesn't seem like it's going anywhere helpful. I think we should stop." In other words, the simple act of noticing creates *just* enough space for choice.

This contrasts with what happens when you are running on autopilot, when you might miss out on saying what is important to you or get stuck in old patterns that aren't productive. Indeed, this is what happened in Molly's situation. When she responded hastily and without present-moment awareness, she lashed out with the same frustration and stubbornness that she was condemning her father for. With mindfulness, she could have taken a step back to say, "Hey, I'm starting to feel frustrated by the direction this is going. Let's press pause so we can be more thoughtful if we choose to continue." In turn, her father might have responded more amenably: "Okay. I'm sorry I upset you."

Chapter 4: *Getting Present Before Diving In*

However, a positive shift is not guaranteed. It is entirely possible that the other person still won't react favorably. In Molly's situation, her father might have responded to the invitation to pause by continuing to explain his point of view: "Look, all I'm trying to say is that people should stop telling me what to do when they don't understand." If this happens, you are not obligated to continue the conversation. Patterns of behavior develop for a reason—because of practice. It can be easy to fall back into them, especially when the other person is also being pulled out of the present moment and into their own patterns. The strategy to "notice" and "communicate" is not something you only do once, but something you can come back to again and again in the span of a single conversation. If needed, be a broken record and reiterate what you've already communicated. It may take several times for the other person to truly hear it. If Molly's father did continue to push the conversation forward, she could say, "I'm going to need to step away from the conversation right now. I love you, and I don't want to end up yelling or fighting."

The other person's response is, in some ways, irrelevant—the purpose of using mindfulness during a difficult conversation is to give *yourself* the space to think and respond in a way that you can feel proud of, rather than letting your emotions take the wheel. This sets you up to use mindfulness in preparation for future conversations.

To practice, think back to a time when you were caught off guard by a difficult conversation. What was the conversation about? Were you able to stay calm and composed in the heat of the moment? Or did your emotions get the best of you? Describe what happened here.

_____
_____
_____
_____
_____

SAYING THE **WRONG** THING

Try to remember what you might have been thinking and feeling in the moment. If you had taken a moment to notice what was going on internally, what might you have noticed about your body, emotions, and thoughts?

_____
_____
_____
_____
_____

Thinking back to what you actually said or didn't say during the conversation, is there anything you wish you'd been able to communicate differently? What would you have said and done in the moment if you had time and space to choose thoughtfully? How might you have said it differently?

_____
_____
_____
_____
_____

How might noticing and communicating in this way have altered the outcome of this situation?

_____
_____
_____
_____
_____

When You Want to Plan for a Future Conversation

You might be wondering, *Wait, I thought you said mindfulness is about being in the present moment. How can you be in the present while also planning for the future?* Mindfulness is indeed about being in the here and now, but sometimes it can be valuable to consider

Chapter 4: Getting Present Before Diving In

the past or future. There is much value in looking to our past to reminisce fondly or learn from our mistakes. Similarly, it is crucial to plan for the future if we want to achieve more complicated long-term goals. It is possible to engage mindfully with both.

Problems arise when you are so preoccupied with the past or future—too busy hanging out in your own mind—that you are unable to live the life you have in front of you. But intentionally examining these imagined realities to learn and grow is not the same as getting stuck in them. For example, consider a person who is planning to talk to their partner about potentially having children. Without mindfulness, the person may ruminate on their partner's past comments and behaviors, trying to guess what their response will be. Or they may anxiously imagine how the conversation could go wrong. None of this is helpful. Alternatively, the person could take a few deep breaths and try to recall difficult discussions the two of them have had in the past, thinking through what went well and what didn't. They can then use this information to better prepare for the future conversation. This act of flexibly shifting your attention—shifting from exploring the past to refocusing on the present—is the practice of mindfulness.

There are also things you can do in the present moment to help prepare you for future conversations, such as reflecting on your internal experiences and clarifying your values. Taking the same example about family planning, the person could notice what thoughts, feelings, and sensations come up when they think about having children. Perhaps they feel anxious about making mistakes, their muscles tense up when thinking about their own parents and childhood, or they have thoughts about why becoming a parent feels so important. These same experiences are likely to be present, and potentially even amplified, during the conversation itself, and reflecting on them beforehand can make them easier to notice when they come up. In doing so, that person can ensure those same values are driving their behavior in the future.

For many of us, having meaningful relationships and being ourselves are important values that make life worth living. Strife, disagreement, and difficult conversations are unavoidable aspects of being in relationships, and learning to navigate these kindly, but assertively, is a primary objective of this book.

With this in mind, we invite you to imagine a difficult conversation that you need or would like to have in the future. This can be something small and manageable or something big and aspirational. It could also be a conversation that you wish you'd had when the opportunity arose.

SAYING THE WRONG THING

Who is it that you want to communicate with? What is the problem or topic of the conversation?

___

Why is it important for you to express your point of view about this? What values are driving your desire to show up, even if you might say the wrong thing? What kind of person do you want to be and what do you want to stand for, even if it means being uncomfortable?

___

When you think about approaching or confronting this person or situation, what happens for you? How does your body react? What emotions show up? What thoughts run through your mind?

___

Take a moment to circle any judgment words you notice in your response. Remember, these tend to be extreme appraisals involving concepts like "right" or "wrong," "should" or "shouldn't," "good" or "bad." These types of judgments tend to interfere with effective communication because they are often emotionally charged and difficult to detach from.

Chapter 4: *Getting Present Before Diving In*

Notice any stories your mind is telling you about how the other person will respond, what will go wrong, what the outcome might be, or how others will view you if you do or don't speak up.

_____
_____
_____
_____
_____

Now, come up with at least two alternative outcomes for what might happen if you have this conversation. They can be simple or elaborate. The idea is to be flexible.

_____
_____
_____
_____
_____

When you know that a specific conversation will happen, remember to (1) mindfully explore past experiences and future possibilities (returning gently to the present when you notice yourself lingering too long), (2) reflect on the internal experiences you have in the moment when you're thinking about the conversation to better prepare for the future, and (3) clarify the values you hold here and now to ensure they guide your behavior during the conversation. Equipped with this information, you may even be able to start communicating ahead of time, setting the stage for success.

Here are some examples of how you can begin to articulate your intentions, ideas, and fears clearly and respectfully:

"I want to have a conversation about ____."

"It's important to me because ____."

"I'm concerned about ____."

"To address this, I think we should agree to ____."

Here are some examples of how you might communicate what you are noticing in the moment:

"I'm starting to feel frustrated/defensive/activated. I think we should take a break."

"I'm feeling embarrassed or uneasy about something I just said. Can we slow down to talk about that?"

Mindfulness from Beginning to End

Mindfulness doesn't have to end just because a conversation is over. Reflecting about a past conversation can give you insight into the future. Your mindfulness skills may also come in handy if you find yourself ruminating on the conversation or aspects of it that you wish had gone differently. If you find yourself replaying the conversation over and over again in your head, this might be a sign that you haven't yet identified or noticed something important about your experience. Perhaps you're scared of what the conversation's outcome will mean for your future, or maybe you're embarrassed that you couldn't break out of old patterns.

By noticing and acknowledging those deeper feelings, you can make sure that your actions aren't driven by them. If there are specific aspects of the conversation that would be useful to acknowledge or clarify with the person after the fact, it is reasonable to communicate those directly. But if you find yourself trying to imagine different outcomes that cannot be changed, it's a good sign that it's time to return to the present, as often as needed.

Finally, mindfulness techniques are not only useful for noticing our own reactions and needs. They are also valuable for observing others and conjecturing about how they may feel or what they may need. Of course, you cannot always know what another person is experiencing internally, but you may be able to notice relevant signs. For example, you might notice that the other person is getting sweaty, that their voice is shakier, or that their posture has become more tense. Grounded in the present, you might notice subtle shifts in their tone of voice that illustrate how they are feeling. You may even be able to pick out when they are using judgment words, or lots of "shoulds" and "shouldn'ts" that indicate they are feeling stuck. When appropriate, it may be useful to communicate what you've noticed and to check in on their experience.

Chapter 4: *Getting Present Before Diving In*

Remember, mindfulness involves active present-moment awareness and is not always a "Zen" or pleasant experience. The utility lies in being in touch with reality *as it is* rather than how you would like it to be. This allows you to respond more honestly and authentically to what is actually happening and can foster a deep sense of connection to yourself and to others.

Play and Practice

- Set a gentle alarm to go off every hour for one day. Each time the alarm goes off, stop what you're doing and take a few mindful breaths, noticing the sensation of being present. If you have a journal, reflect at the end of the day on how this felt and whether it changed your day in any meaningful ways.

- Think ahead to your week. Are there any challenging conversations you will need to have or tense environments you will be in? Identify any likely stress points and set a reminder to use a mindfulness technique such as *Grounding with the Five Senses* or *Square Breathing* before and after the event or conversation. Reflect on whether this practice changed any aspect of the situation compared to what you expected.

- Think of a challenging topic that you may need to discuss in the future and practice role-playing this conversation with a trusted person using the steps outlined in this chapter. Discuss what it was like to be fully present with each other. What was different or the same from how you usually interact with others?

Takeaway Points

- Mindfulness is one aspect of psychological flexibility that involves connecting to the present moment.

- Mindfulness is about nonjudgmentally and intentionally paying attention to what is going on right here, right now.

- Mindfulness is not always relaxing or pleasant. It is an honest appraisal of what is there.

- You can use your breath, physical body, emotions, and thoughts to return to the present moment.

- You can use mindfulness in the moment when a difficult conversation takes you by surprise, or you can use it ahead of time to prepare for difficult conversations in the future.

CHAPTER 5

Finding Your "Why"

> If I lose my direction, I have to look for the North Star, and I go to the north. That does not mean I expect to arrive at the North Star, I just want to go in that direction.
>
> —Thich Nhat Hanh

In chapter 1, we provided you with *our* rationale for this workbook: We wanted to help our clients, colleagues, friends, and family (ourselves included!) practice showing up to challenging conversations more authentically and confidently, especially in the service of social progress and advocacy. Some of those reasons probably fit with your own experiences, but let's use those blossoming mindfulness skills to really reflect on *your* "why" for reading this book. Showing up in difficult conversations can take a lot of work. If you are not clear on *why* you are going through all this work in the first place, it will be that much harder to stand firm, and you'll be much more likely to continue the convenient, yet painful, habit of avoidance. That's why, in this chapter, we will help you gain clarity on why you are here.

With that in mind, take some time to reflect on the following questions, allowing your thoughts to flow unfiltered and without judgment. Take a slow, intentional breath to center yourself before starting.

Why are you reading this book?

_____
_____
_____

SAYING THE *WRONG* THING

What do you want to change in your life by reading this book?
_____
_____
_____

Whom or what are you thinking about most as you read these pages?
_____
_____
_____

What do you want to learn from this workbook?
_____
_____
_____

If someone were to read your answers to the previous four questions, without knowing anything else about you, what would they imagine you care most about in life?
_____
_____
_____

    Your answers to these questions will serve as an anchor for the remainder of your work in both this book and your life. We call this anchor your consciously held **values**. We realize that *values* has become a bit of a pop psychology term in recent years, much like *authenticity* and *self-care*. You may have seen videos online encouraging you to make job or relationship choices based on your values, but with little clarity on the meaning of the word.

Right now, how would you define *values* based on what you've seen and heard so far in your life?
_____
_____
_____

Chapter 5: *Finding Your "Why"*

In this chapter, we will share what values mean to us, describe how you can understand and define your own values, and explain why connecting with your values is important in the context of difficult conversations.

What Are Values?

In ACT, we define values as guiding principles that help us make decisions about who we are and how we want to live our lives. Our values can shift and evolve across time, and we likely hold different values in different areas of our lives. For example, we may value productivity and achievement in our younger years but come to value community, health, and stability as we get older. Similarly, while we may hold values like authenticity and care in our personal relationships, when it comes to paid work or community engagement, our values may take a different shape, such as integrity, openness, or witnessing.

Our values reflect the type of sibling, parent, friend, community member, or partner we want to be. In contrast to goals, which have a clearly defined endpoint that can be reached, it is useful to think of values as *directions* that move with us, guiding us through the ups and downs of life. Values are meant to bring direction, not necessarily bring us happiness or even make our lives easier. In fact, sometimes being aware of our values can actually make life seem harder. For example, when we introduce values to our clients in therapy, we often hear a long list of "shoulds": "I *should* be more patient." "I *should* be less anxious." "I *should* be more assertive." These judgments can keep people stuck in patterns that are contrary to who they are. So instead of thinking about values as "things to be" or "goals to attain," think of them more as ways of being. Here are some examples:

- I want to be a caring parent to my children.
- I want to be a reliable member of my community.
- I want to use my education to empower people who are disempowered.
- It is important to me that I am honest with myself and others.
- It is important to me to be kind to myself and others.
- Standing for integrity brings meaning to my life.

To help you better understand the concept of values, you can also consider a compass. While a compass is designed to point us in the direction of magnetic north, it does not necessarily tell you what sorts of bumps, turns, and distance may lie between. Nor does it tell you what you will find when you reach your destination, only that you are going in the right direction. Values similarly guide you through the unpredictable turns and nuances of life. To do this, though, you must be aware that you even have a compass and then know how to read it.

Exercise—**Values Billboard**

Let's do a quick exercise to warm up your values-identifying muscles. Imagine your city is constructing a billboard on the side of the road. On the left side of the billboard will be a picture of your face (yes, yours!). Since you are going to have to see this billboard somewhat regularly, imagine a picture of yourself that you like or that you feel accurately captures your personality. Once you choose a picture, hold that image in your mind (or really lean in by taping or gluing that picture onto the sample billboard we've included here!).

Now, on the right side of the billboard will be three words that reflect your values—nothing else. After all, billboards must get their messages across quickly so that people don't miss them. Take a moment to come up with three words or short phrases that you'd feel good about seeing next to your face every time you pass by. Write those words on the right side of the billboard here. If you're struggling to come up with words, you can look at the example values list to get you thinking:

Chapter 5: *Finding Your "Why"*

Values List

Achievement	Adventure	Authenticity	Beauty	Collaboration
Community	Compassion	Courage	Creativity	Curiosity
Determination	Empathy	Equality	Fairness	Family
Freedom	Friendship	Growth	Happiness	Health
Honesty	Humor	Independence	Integrity	Joy
Justice	Kindness	Knowledge	Love	Loyalty
Mindfulness	Openness	Passion	Peace	Perseverance
Pleasure	Recognition	Resilience	Respect	Responsibility
Self-Care	Service	Simplicity	Spirituality	Strength
Trust	Understanding	Unity	Wisdom	Wonder

Now that you have your three words or phrases next to your picture, imagine walking or driving by the billboard. What thoughts or feelings come up when you see it? Are you proud? Surprised? Amused?

_____

_____

_____

How do you think other people will feel about your billboard? This includes people you are close to, acquaintances, and strangers.

_____

_____

_____

Was it difficult or easy to come up with the words you chose? Do you think you might have chosen the same words five years ago, and are you likely to choose the same words five years in the future?

_____
_____
_____

Are these words regularly or infrequently on your mind? Do you wish that were different?

_____
_____
_____

Do any of these words reflect goals that you could one day complete, or are they more representative of your overall life?

_____
_____
_____

Do you feel pressured by others to embody these attributes, or are they consistent with how you see yourself?

_____
_____
_____

Exercise—Who Do You Want to Be in Difficult Conversations?

When having difficult conversations, it is important that you show up and speak up in a way that allows you to remain true to yourself. This exercise will help you clarify values that are relevant to this process. For this exercise, you may read or follow along using this link so you can fully engage without distraction: www.sayingthewrongthing.com/audio/values.

To begin, take a few slow breaths and allow your body to settle into a posture that's supported, but alert. Recall a recent interaction where you worried about saying the wrong thing. Kindly give yourself permission to not linger on the outcome of that situation.

Chapter 5: *Finding Your "Why"*

Instead, bring your attention to the physical sensations you experienced at the time. Can you recall how your breathing and heart rate felt? What were your muscles doing? Remember to gently breathe as you recall this interaction.

Now turn your attention to the emotions you experienced. Did you feel any anger, fear, or sadness? Welcome these feelings now . . . breathing slowly. What were those emotions telling you was important? Were they letting you know why this conversation was important to you, or were they coming from a place of fear or protection, or perhaps even both? What did these emotions let you know you cared most about? What did they tell you about what made the conversation challenging? Remember to keep breathing in and out.

Now think about the type of person you wanted to be in that exchange. What did you want to embody? It is natural to focus on what you did wrong—or what you didn't do but wish you had—so be gentle and kind as you think back. Was the issue important? Or the relationship? Maybe both? Or something entirely different? Let these reflections about what or who was important inform your choices about how you would like to show up to a conversation like this one. Breathing slowly, ask yourself: *Who do I want to be in this encounter? What do I want to embody?* Again, remember to breathe with kindness and without judgment. Now, answer this question for yourself: *I want to be the kind of person who* _____.

When you're ready, come back into an awareness of your physical body in that supported and alert posture. Gently, and with kindness, come back to the present moment and to the pages of this book, taking one last full breath cycle—in through your nose and out through your mouth with a sigh.

Engaging in slow and mindful reflection on difficult encounters can help reorient your focus toward your values, much like checking a compass, rather than remaining stuck on what didn't go well. It may take some time and continued practice for your values to start to feel clear, but just as physical exercise takes time to build muscle, you are gradually changing the way your brain interacts with difficult experiences. So, nice job working out your brain!

Exercise—Values Bull's-Eye

This exercise will help you get more clarity on where you stand in relation to your values. The first step is to reread your answer to the question we posed at the start of this chapter—Why are you reading this book?—and pick the top four values that you want to focus on while doing this work. For example, maybe it's (1) integrity, (2) family, (3) compassion, and (4) equity. Make sure they are things that matter to you and not just things you are "supposed" to value. Once you have your top values, write them in each of the four quadrants of the following bull's-eye.

Now, take a moment to think about how you have embodied these values lately. Place an X in each quadrant to signify where you fall. An X in the center of the bull's-eye means you have lived this value to the full extent that you want to, while an X in the outer circle means you have been very distant from the value. This is just a check-in with yourself, not an opportunity for judgment or shame. You can only understand where you need to go if you know where you are now.

Now take a different-colored writing utensil and indicate just how important each value is to you. An X near the center of the bull's-eye means it matters more, while an X near the outer circle means it matters less. Not every X needs to be directly in the center; it is likely that some will be closer and others will be farther away.

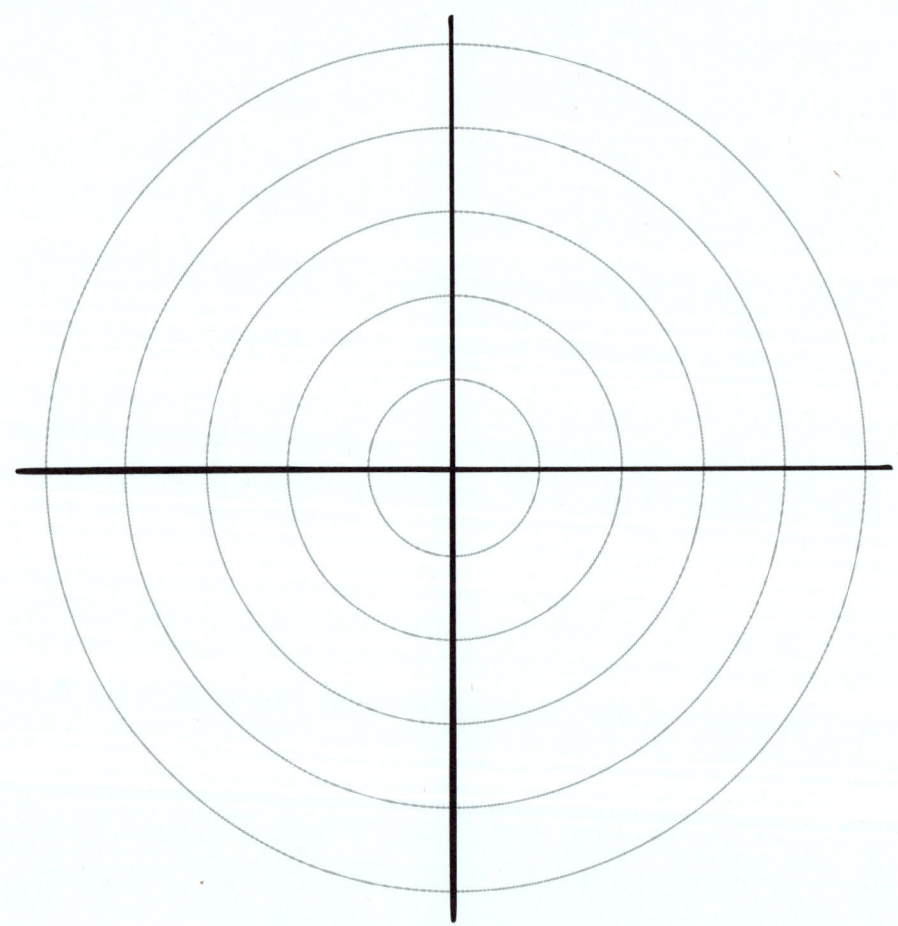

Chapter 5: *Finding Your "Why"*

Finally, take some time to reflect on what you've drawn in the bull's-eye. What is it like to notice the relative closeness or distance of your actions from your values? Do you feel right on target with some or surprised by how far off you have grown? Try to observe these reflections without judgment and invite these emotions to do what they're intended to: motivate change or reinforce existing behaviors.

_____
_____
_____
_____
_____

Why Are Values Important?

When you aren't clear on your values, it can be easy to feel pushed around by the circumstances of your life. In the previous exercise, you may have struggled to identify if what your emotions were telling you was truly important. This is partly due to the rise in digital and social media in recent years, which has us plugged in to other people's ideas and priorities almost constantly. We are immersed in a constant stream of opinions and messaging about what is important in life, often without realizing the extent to which this content influences us. Although being digitally connected has many advantages—for example, we can see life from many perspectives, learn information that was previously inaccessible, and connect with others across great distances—we can easily lose sight of our own priorities. In turn, we may automatically behave according to a set of predetermined rules that aren't actually helpful, without realizing that we have other options.

For example, let's say your coworker, who often pushes your buttons, sees another coworker wearing a Pride shirt and makes an ill-informed comment about "child grooming." Without hesitation, what would your automatic response be? Would you shut down, change the subject, or snap at them with a sharp rebuttal? Often, we don't have time to pause and think in these moments before the rules we've always lived by take over and make choices for us ("I *should* stand up for others," "I *have to* avoid conflict," "I *must* be nice no matter what"). The magic is, we actually *do* have a wide range of choices available to us. In this example, mindfully pausing to connect with your values may give you other options, like expressing curiosity to open a dialogue or sharing your own personal connection to the meaning behind a Pride shirt. Simply put, clarifying your values can help cut through some of the noise.

When you hold your values in conscious awareness, your choices in difficult situations become clearer. You can act in accordance with your values, even if the outcome isn't always ideal. What's more, your everyday actions begin to feel more rewarding (Fields et al., 2022). How nice is that?! You can probably think of a time when you felt true to yourself and how rewarding that feeling was. It's no wonder that living a values-based life is associated with less anxiety and depression (Tunç et al., 2023) and higher resilience (Ceary et al., 2019). It can even buffer against some of the most difficult life experiences, such as chronic racism (Graham et al., 2015) and caring for someone with a terminal illness (Davis et al., 2015), to name a few. In contrast, when you are not aware of your values, or you are but don't act on them, it can feel like you're shuffling through life or living in a state of inner turmoil.

Where Do Values Come From?

None of us live in total isolation. We didn't suddenly spring up from the ground as complete people with fully formed identities and values. We have all been molded by the environments we grew up in and the people who cared for and hurt us. We are also shaped by the time we occupy in history, including the technology available to us, common parenting practices, exposure to global crises, and the availability of economic and natural resources, which naturally change throughout our own lifetimes. How we engage with the world is different from how our parents, grandparents, and other ancestors have, though we are influenced by our heritage and ancestry to some extent.

Indeed, most cultures and religious systems place importance on certain values, from putting family first to caring for those with less than yourself to having a well-formed individual identity. For example, all three of us grew up in the United States, where we have been taught to place importance on individual identity, the pursuit of one's own goals and dreams, and the idea that anything is possible if one works hard enough. There is also a very common value in our society that is not explicitly discussed or idealized: comfort. Americans tend to hold personal comfort as one of the most important pillars upon which to build a life and make crucial decisions. We believe this is one of the biggest hurdles to having difficult but meaningful conversations in our society, as so many of us avoid conflict

Chapter 5: *Finding Your "Why"*

to preserve a sense of personal security and minimize discomfort. No wonder so many of us have difficulty engaging in a balanced and caring conversation!

Given that we can discover our own values throughout life or learn them as part of our heritage and ancestry, we like to think of values as being either inherited or acquired. **Inherited values** are those we learn early in life from social influences, including family members and important community members, while **acquired values** are those that we develop throughout the course of life based on our own experiences. Both types are equally important and can drive our behaviors. Inherited values may not always feel freely chosen, but by bringing awareness to them we are able to choose how these values are reflected in our actions. Acting on values that are instilled in us without ever acknowledging their role can be an example of inflexibility if those values conflict with our other consciously held values. Therefore, take some time in the next exercise to think about how your own ancestry, culture, and family have impacted your values.

Exercise—Examining Your Origins

What are some values you learned directly from your family upbringing?

___

___

___

___

What were the lessons your caregivers emphasized about how to treat people, animals, or the planet?

___

___

___

___

Were you taught certain values or morals as part of a religious or philosophical system? What were they?

_____
_____
_____
_____

What does society, as well as the media to which you are exposed, suggest that you should care about?

_____
_____
_____
_____

What are some prominent world events that have occurred in your lifetime, and how have they shaped your generation's values?

_____
_____
_____
_____

How Do Values Relate to Privilege?

Just as values do not appear out of a vacuum, they also do not exist in isolation from the privilege and positionality that someone holds within society. Privilege refers to the relative advantages someone has in life based on their various identities (e.g., gender, race, ethnicity, religion, education, language, citizenship), whereas positionality is the social position, or status, they hold in society based on these identities. It's important to recognize that our identities do not hold innate power or value; this is determined by how a culture or society prioritizes them. For example, in some cultures, financial wealth is prioritized, while in other cultures, educational prestige is seen as more valuable and desirable.

Chapter 5: *Finding Your "Why"*

If you hold greater privilege or higher status in society, you're not often compelled to think about your inherited values because these values are likely reflective of the "majority." For example, if you are born into a family that values independence and wealth, growing up in a capitalist culture that reinforces those very values may not create any need for reflection or curiosity. In many ways, this is like a fish not realizing water is wet because it's all around them; they have no other point of comparison. On the flip side, if your identities tend to place you in a less powerful societal position, you have probably often considered your own values and cultural heritage. For example, if you are born into a family with strong values of spirituality, growing up in a culture that does not reward religiosity or spirituality might lead you to reflect on where that value comes from and how it fits into your overall identity and place within society.

The following questions can help you think further about how your upbringing and current position within society have shaped the values you hold today.

What are your inherited values? These are the values that were passed on to you by your earliest social influences. Try to list at least three.

_____
_____
_____
_____

Which of these inherited values do you continue to consider important and meaningful today?

_____
_____
_____
_____

Which of these inherited values have you let go of (if any)?

_____
_____
_____
_____

What values have you acquired from personal experience? Try to list at least three.
_____
_____
_____
_____

What emotions are coming up as you reflect on your values?
_____
_____
_____
_____

It can be powerful to understand how your values have been formed and how this process happens within the intertwined web of human connection. How you see yourself, how you see the world around you, and what you deem important can all help you find your "why" for showing up to difficult conversations.

Exercise—Values Clarification

Now that you've gained a deeper understanding of how your values came to be, it's time to fine-tune what you've been working on and really focus on the values you hold across several life domains. Getting clarity on the *multiple* values that guide you can be incredibly useful when you are feeling stuck or in conflict with yourself.

For this exercise, try to identify one or two values that you hold in each category. Remember, values are ways of *being* that guide you in this area of life. Values are important in and of themselves, not necessarily for the results they produce. Watch out for the pull to think of goals here. If you find yourself listing concrete options that you could check off a to-do list, pause and go a little deeper by asking what value that goal may be fulfilling within your core being.

Chapter 5: *Finding Your "Why"*

Relationships: What qualities do you want to embody as a parent, sibling, friend, partner, and so forth?

_____
_____
_____

Physical health: What qualities do you deem important when it comes to your physical body?

_____
_____
_____

Spirituality: Is it important for you to connect to something bigger than yourself? If so, what qualities or characteristics underlie this part of your humanity?

_____
_____
_____

Community: What qualities do you want to bring to society, your country, or your community?

_____
_____
_____

Recreation: What qualities define your restorative and recreational time and choices?

_____
_____
_____

Employment or education: What qualities are important in the work or education choices you make?

_____
_____
_____

Other: What other qualities or characteristics guide your attention and choices in life?

_____
_____
_____

Of the values you listed here, which feel particularly related to showing up in difficult conversations?

_____
_____
_____
_____
_____

Values in Conversation

Sometimes, shedding light on your values can complicate things. When you are in contact with your values, your relationships might change in painful ways; complacency becomes more difficult, and you start making choices in life that require more energy and effort. Difficulty and discomfort, though, are not necessarily bad! (If you don't believe us yet, that's okay; we'll make the case in chapter 6.) Your objective is to develop a healthy relationship with the discomfort that arises when you act on your values. For example, after clarifying for yourself that maintaining communication with your immediate family is important, you might experience discomfort trying to think of the last time you called your sibling. But rather than becoming a source of guilt or sadness, the skills in this chapter can, over time, make that pang of discomfort simply a reminder to pick up the phone.

Chapter 5: *Finding Your "Why"*

Monica's Story—Centering Values to Find my Voice

I work in a small specialty clinic built by and for Asian American Pacific Islander (AAPI) refugee and immigrant communities. As with many specialty nonprofit clinics in the United States, it has been difficult for us to sustain financially. Over the past several years, we have been gradually merging with a larger community behavioral health center in our area, with mostly positive results. This year, however, it was decided that we would be fully absorbed, meaning our name would change and we would no longer operate under our own leadership. Most of my coworkers—who share identities with our service population and in many cases have personal experiences of trauma and identity erasure—felt that our work and team culture were being erased, whitewashed, and microaggressed against. There were several instances of higher-ups handing down changes that were unworkable for our clients and hurtful to our staff.

I am the only white staff member in our clinic—all of the new leadership team share this racial identity—and I deeply value integrity and social justice. I was overcome with anxiety and anger for months, grappling with our sudden loss of agency and how to use my positionality without speaking over anyone. I tried my best to ask questions in meetings and point to the pain being experienced, with very little impact. Eventually, I asked to meet with the director of diversity, equity, and inclusion (DEI) and a human resources representative. I wanted to go into that meeting spewing fire, pointing out hypocrisies, and demanding an action plan, but I knew that would only have pushed them into a defensive stance. Instead, I took time to write out the issues I was witnessing, connected to my breath, and reminded myself of my values—of why it was important that I engage in this dialogue.

In turn, I remembered that I find it important to embody integrity and kindness in difficult conversations, that I want to move in the direction of creating an equitable work climate, and that I want to be the sort of person who demonstrates qualities of honesty and openness. I was received with respect and told that my concerns would be brought to the executive team. While I did not see this meeting have an immediate impact, I like to believe it contributed to leadership's understanding of the clear discontent on our team and led to their eventual shift in tone and approach to changes. I feel proud of how I stepped up for my coworkers and our clients, and how I used my positionality to speak in the corporate language that would be heard. Even if I don't know how much of an impact I actually had, now I know I can do this again and again if I need to.

SAYING THE *WRONG* THING

As you can see from Monica's story, acting on your values is not always a straightforward path. For her, it took several attempts over the course of months to determine how to have the greatest impact. She also did not get to see immediate results. But she learned what she is capable of, and she allowed her values to guide her in having some vulnerable conversations.

However, as humans, we have a finite amount of energy, and engaging in *every* difficult conversation that presents itself would be unsustainable. By clarifying your values, you can direct your energy to the dialogues with the highest potential impact—to those that will bring you the most meaning and fulfillment. Just because a conversation (or anything else) is challenging does not necessarily mean it is important. Only you can choose which conversations are worth having.

Mahmood's Story—The Fear of Living Out Values

For many Muslims in the United States who posted about the Hamas-led attack on Israel in the fall of 2023 and Israel's subsequent response against Gaza, doing so was an important way to use their voices, raise awareness, and showcase their solidarity. Unfortunately, this often came with consequences like losing friends who backed Israel's response, being blocked by social media platforms, or even being mislabeled as an anti-Semite or a racist. For years, I've seen this dynamic wreak havoc within the Muslim community and beyond, with multiple friends and peers being falsely labeled as anti-Semitic and even losing their jobs after speaking their truth.

As Israel intensified its war on Gaza, resulting in hundreds and then thousands of mostly women and children being killed, I desperately wanted to lend my voice to the anti-war ceasefire movement as well. But I was paralyzed with fear of being falsely smeared online or losing close friends who supported Israel's war. However, after continued discussions with people I respect, I decided to post something on social media in line with my values. As a new father, I value creating a safe environment for all children. As a former journalist, I value the importance of speaking truth to power. And as an anti-war advocate, I value prioritizing peace above all else.

While creating these posts, I centered my message and narrative to be in line with these values. I also did ample research to strengthen my stance against and prepare for personal attacks or trolling. I ended up posting three messages over the course of a weekend. For my first values-oriented post, I showcased a child at the edge of his life being rushed to the hospital to highlight the brutal devastation against children in the conflict. For my second values-oriented post, I talked about how a historic number of Palestinian journalists have been targeted or killed and how this has impacted their

Chapter 5: *Finding Your "Why"*

> ability to share important stories and perspectives with the world. And finally, I reposted a protest speech by a prominent American Jewish peace organization.
>
> Thankfully, the overwhelming response to the posts was positive. Then, to my surprise, my wife expressed concerns about the first post featuring the image of a hurt child. While she understood the impetus, she felt strongly that she would hate for our child's picture to be used in the same way. I was glad she shared her concerns with me, as we hold similar values and ethics, and it gave me an opportunity to reflect. In the end, I agreed with her assessment, and I ended up taking down that one post as a result.
>
> Afterward, I felt good about my approach to this. I waited for more negative feedback, but it never came. Despite anticipatory anxiety and some real-time discomfort, by creating content and messages in line with my values, I felt empowered to continue advocating for peace in the future months. I went on to use and refine the following approach, not just in social media but in opinion pieces, podcasts, and one-on-one discussions with other people.

Mahmood's Exercise—Clarifying Values in the Face of Fears

Think of something you have wanted to say or do but have not yet been able to due to fears about how others will react. This could be anything from correcting a relative for saying something that is no longer considered acceptable to speaking up in a larger context where there are power differentials. Go through the following prompts to clarify the role of your values and identify actions that may help you overcome your fears.

First, describe the scenario. What is it that you are afraid to do or say?

_____
_____
_____
_____
_____
_____

SAYING THE WRONG THING

Why does saying or doing something in this scenario matter to you? What kind of attributes are you hoping to embody? What would it mean to you if you were able to take action? What might it mean to others? Spend a moment reflecting on your values.

_____
_____
_____
_____
_____
_____

What scares you about the idea of saying or doing something in this scenario? Is it a fear of rejection? Fear of losing a job? Fear of being physically harmed? Do you feel like your fears are likely to occur? Or is it that they feel unlikely, but the stakes are too high to take a chance? Spend a moment reflecting on your fears.

_____
_____
_____
_____
_____
_____

Considering your reflections so far, identify up to three specific fears that are either the most likely to occur or feel the most consequential:

1. _____
2. _____
3. _____

Thinking about the values you identified above, as well as your fears, does it feel worth it to move forward with action? Perhaps the consequences outweigh the values, or you realize your initial motivation is not actually in line with your values but reflects outside pressure. If that's the case, stop the exercise here and consider starting over with a new

Chapter 5: *Finding Your "Why"*

scenario. But if you determine that it *is* worth acting on even in the face of your fears, make a plan using this template:

The action I am going to take is: _____

The worst-case scenario outcome would be: _____

If the worst occurs, I will: _____

If other negative consequences happen, I will: _____

Taking a thoughtful, values-based approach to action means evaluating your plan and adjusting it as needed. Question your assumptions and imagine different potential outcomes than you might expect. Consider doing additional research or talking to someone you trust. Edit your plan as needed before acting. If you do act, reflect on how it went and what you could have done differently.

_____
_____
_____
_____
_____
_____

Avoiding difficult conversations is sometimes healthy. We never want you to put yourself in danger just because you feel like you need to adhere to your values. If a situation feels unsafe emotionally, physically, or otherwise, tend to your safety first before deciding how you want to act on your values. That being said, pain and discomfort do not automatically signify a lack of safety. You'll learn in the next chapter how easy it can be to misinterpret discomfort for danger and how this can keep you stuck.

SAYING THE *WRONG* THING

Play and Practice

- As you progress through this workbook, continue to return to the questions you answered at the start of this chapter. Notice whether your answers change or become more detailed. It is especially important to return to these questions when you are struggling with motivation or feeling lost in the possibilities of what could go wrong.

- Start building a *Values Compass* using the template provided at the end of this chapter. Identify your top eight most important values, ranking them in order of importance. Write the top four values at each of the long points (where north, south, east, and west would normally be labeled), and your next four most important values at each of the shorter points between where the cardinal directions would be. Feel free to use the values list we provided on page 85 or come up with your own words. You can get creative and use different colors or designs when filling in your compass. Take note of (and potentially highlight, bold, or use a distinct color for) the values that are particularly relevant to relationships and communication. Use the blank space around the compass to jot down reminders or sayings that help you connect with the values you've identified. Revisit your compass when preparing for important conversations or any other time you need a reminder of what matters most.

- Talk with a trusted person about the values you've identified in this chapter. Ask about their inherited and acquired values and see what you learn about each other. Take this a step further by discussing your inherited values with a family member. Did you inherit the same values? What may have influenced any differences?

- Identify at least two values related to difficult conversations and practice taking small steps in the direction of those values. Maybe it's practicing openness toward someone you disagree with. Maybe it's finding the courage to speak up in conversations you would normally feel too insecure about. Write about the challenges or rewards you encounter when taking these small steps.

Chapter 5: *Finding Your "Why"*

> ## Takeaway Points
>
> - Values highlight who you want to be in different areas of your life. You can think of values as a compass pointing you in the direction of an intentional life well-lived.
>
> - Values are *not* goals with a clearly defined endpoint. Values can change with time.
>
> - The social contexts in which you grew up and currently live can both impact value formation. Some values are inherited while others are acquired.
>
> - Values can sometimes feel like they conflict with one another. Bringing conscious awareness to what matters to you can help shape your behavior in these situations.
>
> - Not all conversations are worth having—and some may even feel unsafe. Your values can help you make meaningful decisions in those situations.

Values Compass

CHAPTER 6

The Unintended Cost of Control

> "Try to pose for yourself this task: not to think of a polar bear, and you will see that the cursed thing will come to mind every minute."
>
> —Fyodor Dostoyevsky

The benefits of living a mindful and values-based life may seem clear, but it can be difficult for many people to put their values into action in the here and now. Maybe you've found this to be the case for yourself. Have you ever wondered why? How can it be that you struggle to implement things that are crucially important to the kind of person you would like to be? Why is it so hard? What gets in the way?

It turns out that there are several uniquely human experiences that get in the way of being mindful and living consistently with your values. This includes biological factors (such as the human ability for metacognition) and social factors (such as the prevalence of toxic positivity). In this chapter, we examine these factors in greater detail and describe how they can contribute to uncomfortable thoughts, sensations, and emotions that make it hard to speak out in difficult conversations—even when staying silent goes against your values.

Metacognition and Our Incredible Imaginations

Most animals see and process the stimuli that are right in front of them: A dog becomes excited by the smells and sights on a walk, distracted by every new and novel sensation (squirrel!). The dog doesn't wonder, *Does my owner love me?* or *Should I conserve my energy in case we go on another walk later?* In many ways, their ignorance is blissfully focused on the present moment. Humans, on the other hand, can envision the past and the future as well as metacognate, or think about our thinking. We can walk around in memories of years past, relishing or agonizing in every detail. We can vividly paint a future scenario that has never happened and feel as though we are there. We can be aware that we are existing in the past or future and then judge or commend ourselves for it. And miraculously, when we entertain the past or imagine the future, our bodies respond physiologically, as if we are experiencing these events in the here and now! Surely you have experienced physical anxiety, such as nausea and increased heart rate, while imagining some cringeworthy memory or possible future interaction. To illustrate this point, we invite you to participate in the following brief experiential practice.

Exercise—Lemon

For this exercise, you may read or follow along using this link so you can fully engage without distraction: www.sayingthewrongthing.com/audio/lemon.

Start by beginning to deepen your breath, allowing your eyes to softly focus on a spot in front of you. Gently breathe in . . . and out. Begin to feel gravity pull the weight of your body toward the earth as you settle into the present moment. And with the next exhale, go ahead and allow your eyes to close if you feel safe to do so, or let them rest on something neutral that won't distract you.

Now, envision in your mind's eye a bright, ripe lemon. Examine it with curiosity, as though it's the first time you've encountered such a thing. You might begin by imagining what it is like to hold this lemon in your hand . . . feeling the cool, waxy skin against your palm . . . rolling the fruit in your hands to feel its weight . . . noticing its dimpled skin, size, shape. You might also notice its color, observing the way its shade of yellow differs with each contour or as you turn it beneath the light.

Imagine bringing the lemon to your nose and inhaling deeply to notice what you smell. Perhaps you can detect faint citrus oils. Imagine digging your nails into the skin of the

Chapter 6: *The Unintended Cost of Control*

lemon, noticing how the scent changes. Does it amplify? Does it come with any memories? How does the texture of the skin change as you do this?

Now, holding the lemon in both hands, imagine that you break the fruit open into two pieces. Perhaps you can hear the fruit splitting as you do so. Notice the sensation of the juice running down your hands or arms. Notice if the scent permeates the air. Look at the inside of the fruit and observe what you see. How do the colors change? What does the inner pulp look like? Describe its texture. Appreciate the incredible change this fruit can undergo.

Now, imagine bringing the lemon to your mouth and nose, taking a moment to deeply inhale. How does the scent differ from before the fruit was opened? Do you notice any changes in your body? Go ahead and imagine taking a bite of the lemon pulp. What happens? Do you salivate? Does your stomach rumble? What does the lemon taste like? What happens as you chew? Does your face change in response? Do memories come to mind?

Take these last few moments to release the image of the lemon. Notice how you feel as you begin to deepen your breath once more. Imagine your body in the space you're in, feeling the weight of gravity once again grounding you to the earth. And when you're ready, allow your eyes to gently open.

Take a moment here to document what you noticed from this practice.

General observations:

_____

_____

_____

Visual observations:

_____

_____

_____

Tactile observations:

_____

_____

_____

SAYING THE *WRONG* THING

Olfactory observations:
_____
_____
_____

Taste observations:
_____
_____
_____

Most people are astounded to find that simply envisioning the experience of holding, smelling, and tasting a lemon can invoke physical sensations that mimic its actual presence. You may have been able to easily conjure the sight, smell, taste, and feel of the lemon, resulting in reactionary salivation, a puckered facial expression, and a rumbling stomach—all for something that was not physically present, something that was not real in this moment. How incredible is that?

However, there is a flip side: Just as we can vividly imagine a neutral or enjoyable experience that is not real, so too can we imagine a painful memory or feared outcome with the same intensity. When this happens, the impulse for most of us is to try to escape the discomfort in some way. This reflects an evolutionary mechanism known as the "fight, flight, freeze, or fawn" response, which is intended to keep us safe. This well-established physiological response to distress has been hardwired into our brains since the origin of humanity. So, when we're faced with a threat—whether real or perceived—we can take one of the following actions:

- **Fight:** We fight back against the perceived threat by yelling, lashing out at others, arguing aggressively, or even physically fighting.

- **Flight:** We run away from the threat to preserve our safety. This can look like fidgeting, having trouble being still, trying to ignore the threat, or leaving the space.

- **Freeze:** We become immobile and "play dead" to avoid drawing attention to ourselves. This occurs when the threat is perceived as so emotionally and physically overwhelming that we cannot escape. This can look like checking out or glazing over.

Chapter 6: *The Unintended Cost of Control*

- **Fawn:** We attempt to appease the threat with flattery, ignoring our own needs or feigning agreement. This might look like smiling and nodding, laughing, or agreeing, despite feeling something incongruent inside. While these behaviors appear more relational than those previously listed, they are nonetheless automatic responses that are not freely chosen.

When the "fight, flight, freeze, or fawn" response is activated, the brain's decision-making center (the prefrontal cortex) goes offline, while the brain's emotional control center (the amygdala) goes into overdrive. That means when we're faced with a threat, our capacity for logical reasoning and rational thought decreases. And that's a good thing! In the face of danger, we don't want to be wondering what to make for dinner or weighing the pros and cons of our actions; we want to be responding quickly and automatically in a potentially life-saving manner. In the context of escaping a wild and ferocious animal, this response is highly adaptive in maximizing our chances for survival. The problem with this strategy is that it gets overapplied when there is no real threat, causing us to avoid (or flee from) *all* difficult thoughts and feelings—rather than only those that are objectively dangerous.

When it comes to living a values-based life, we are often faced with imagined threats related specifically to the things we care most about. Think for a moment about some of the human experiences we find most painful, such as grief, betrayal, failure, rejection, or guilt. These experiences all have one very important thing in common: They can only occur when something important is on the line. Grief may be the clearest example, as it is—by definition—a reaction to losing something or someone we hold dear. Betrayal and rejection occur when someone important to us does not feel the same regard for us in return. Failure and guilt can arise when we do not live up to or act consistently with what we have decided matters. In fact, most negative emotions (such as anger, sadness, doubt, disappointment, jealousy, and regret) can usually be traced back to something meaningful or important.

For this reason, responding to these kinds of experiences with the same fight-flight-freeze-fawn responses as we do to physical threats can get in the way of living a mindful and values-based life. For example, if your response to rejection is to lash out (fight), you may push others further away. Similarly, if your response to self-doubt is to shut down (freeze), you will be less likely to reach goals and have feelings of accomplishment. If your response to grief is to avoid all reminders of your loss (flight), you can miss out on opportunities to process and heal, in addition to all the important things and people you might be inadvertently avoiding as a result. And if your response to a disrespectful comment is to smile and laugh lightly (fawn), there is no opportunity for growth or change in the relationship and your self-respect may diminish.

Societal Expectations and Toxic Positivity

It is not just our overactive imaginations that can interfere with the ability to live a mindful, values-based life; societal expectations get in the way as well. So many of us have been conditioned by our culture, our family, our religion, or the media to believe that feeling sad, anxious, upset, or angry is "bad." We have come to believe that "wellness" equals the absence of upsetting emotions and the presence of only unbridled happiness. As a result, when "bad" emotions show up, many of us have learned to avoid or struggle against them. We call this the *control* (or *avoidance*) *agenda*. Unfortunately, living a life that is devoid of discomfort is not the reality of human existence. It is normal for people to feel the full range of emotions, including those that are uncomfortable.

To illustrate the difficulties with trying to push away or suppress challenging experiences, let's try a brief experiment. Think back to the last time you felt upset, annoyed, or frustrated. This might include a time when you encountered a minor inconvenience or when you went through a more significant disruption in your life. Where were you? What were you doing? Was anyone else there? Spend a moment remembering the details of the situation, including what you could see, hear, smell, and even feel around you.

Now, delete that memory from your mind.

No, we're not joking. We want you to try as hard as you can to erase the memory. Try as many strategies as you can think of. If you don't think there's any way to delete it in such a short amount of time, do you think you could delete it by the end of the week if given the chance? What if you were extremely motivated? If someone offered you one million dollars to delete the memory, could you do it then? Get creative and jot down your best idea for deleting the memory by the end of the week and becoming one million dollars richer (humor us!).

Best memory deletion strategy:

_____

_____

_____

Chapter 6: *The Unintended Cost of Control*

What do you think about the idea you came up with? How likely it is to work? Here are a few examples of the creative responses our workshop participants have come up with:

- Spend the whole week journaling about every other memory possible to try to override it (time-consuming, but maybe worth it for the money).

- Consume enough alcohol to be confused and convince yourself it never happened (questionable whether this counts as deleting, but we'll allow it for the purposes of this thought experiment, though it's inadvisable).

- Try to sustain a concussion (highly inadvisable).

- Do nothing and forget about it (this one is not very creative, but it did come up the most often).

Do you think your strategy would be more or less effective than these? Maybe you think doing nothing and forgetting is the best way to go, and it probably is (certainly less dangerous than some of the others!). But do you believe you could really forget something in one week with one million dollars on the line? That alone would make it hard to forget!

While the futility of this exercise might be obvious (thank you for humoring us), we offer it here to illustrate why it is so problematic that society has conditioned us to push away uncomfortable experiences. As much as we may be tempted or encouraged to try erasing these experiences from our memories, this is a nearly impossible task. Nevertheless, phrases like "Cheer up!" "Just don't think about it!" and "Mind over matter!" are deeply woven into our everyday conversations, inspirational social media posts, and even some therapy modalities. Positivity and positive thinking are not themselves negative (and can certainly be useful!), but they become problematic when they are used to control and avoid unwanted experiences. These "thought stoppers" or "positive thinking" tools all suggest that we have the power to change our internal experiences, but this memory deletion exercise is a simple reminder of just how ineffective and harmful this belief can be. At best, we might waste a week journaling when we could be doing other more important things—and at worst, we could end up with a concussion!

SAYING THE *WRONG* THING

Jess's Story—Someone to Bear Witness

Maybe you've lost a job. Maybe you or a loved one received a scary health diagnosis. Maybe a relationship that you believed would last for life has come to an end. We've all had moments of hardship when life did not go as planned. Whether or not we remember the details of the event, we often remember how the people around us reacted when we looked for support.

When I was just out of graduate school, I had an extremely stressful job that required me to be on call twenty-four hours a day, five to seven days a week. I was also paid half of what a full year of social work school costs. I was struggling with poor sleep, decreased mood, and regular episodes of tearfulness. I could never relax, even when doing things I love, like seeing live music. I sought advice from mentors, friends, and my partner at the time. Almost universally, responses were well-intentioned, but felt dismissive:

"There must be some positives."

"That's hard, but I'm sure you're learning from the process?"

"This is just one step in the journey."

"You need to grind a little at the beginning to get where you want to go. Keep your head up."

Finally, a friend listened to my frustrations and asked if I just needed to vent, if I needed someone to bear witness, or if I was looking for solutions. By framing their response in this way, they communicated that they recognized my distress, but they wanted to be there in a way that would be most helpful for me in the moment. While positive thinking can allow us to take a different perspective on an event or tap into a well of resilience, it is not always what we need. Toxic positivity raises the stakes to the next level and becomes almost an automated response, which can interfere with the ability to move through a situation to find a solution.

Jess's Exercise—Toxic Positivity Trash Can

Toxic positivity involves going to unhealthy extremes to maintain a positive or optimistic outlook on life. With toxic positivity, you minimize or ignore uncomfortable, negative, or distressing emotions with statements like "Everything happens for a reason!" and "Don't worry, be happy." This stunts your ability to experience these normal and useful components of being a person—and it also results in the pressure to be constantly happy regardless of your unique life circumstances.

Chapter 6: *The Unintended Cost of Control*

For this exercise, fill this trash can up with toxically positive phrases you've heard or have used yourself. Some examples might be:

"Look on the bright side."

"Everything happens for a reason."

"The past is in the past."

"Just think about something else."

When you were writing down these phrases, what feelings came up for you? Common responses include anger, resentment, guilt, or even relief.

_____
_____
_____
_____
_____

SAYING THE *WRONG* THING

Think about a situation where you found yourself saying some of these phrases to yourself. What thoughts or feelings do you think you might have been avoiding?

_____
_____
_____
_____
_____

Why might it be important or functional for you to experience these thoughts or feelings? What are they trying to tell you? What is the cost of continuing to avoid them?

_____
_____
_____
_____
_____

Not only is toxic positivity harmful, but when you try to suppress or ignore your emotions and thoughts, you tend to amplify the very sensations you were struggling to get rid of in the first place! This phenomenon is called "ironic process theory." It was first demonstrated in an experiment in which subjects followed the prompt "don't think about a white bear," ironically resulting in higher rates of intrusive thoughts about white bears (Wegner et al., 1987). This effect has subsequently been replicated in many different contexts, but had already been a documented phenomenon for hundreds of years. (Just look back to the Dostoyevsky quote—from 1863!—that we included at the start of this chapter.) But check your own experience: Try not thinking about a white bear for the next sixty seconds. Even if you are marginally successful, chances are you had to repeatedly cue yourself about the prompt, so you effectively *were* thinking about a white bear, much like our memory deletion experiment.

Chapter 6: *The Unintended Cost of Control*

The Control Agenda

Let's put together what you've learned so far. Your incredible imagination and metacognition allow you to envision in detail things and events that are not happening in the present moment. These abilities allow for innovation, creativity, and progress, but there's also a catch. Your body is wired to respond to threats quickly and intensely, which is useful in the face of clear and present danger. But when your mind brings imagined threats into the present moment, your body can respond similarly, whether or not danger actually exists—you may respond to negative emotions with fight, flight, freeze, or fawn reactions even when these strategies are not only unhelpful but also exacerbate the experience (just like the white bear!). When you respond to imagined threats in the same way as physical danger, your brain is essentially attempting to control the uncontrollable. And none of this is helped by the fact that society is trying to convince you that negative emotions are particularly threatening and to be avoided at all costs. What a conundrum!

When you also remember that negative emotions are usually directly related to something important to you, it's no wonder living a mindful and values-based life is much more easily said than done. This is the universal challenge we are all faced with. Take a moment to remember a time you felt emotional pain, such as disappointment, anxiety, or grief. As before, this might be a minor inconvenience you experienced or a time when you went through a more significant life event. Feel free to use the scenario from earlier that you tried (we assume unsuccessfully) to delete from your memory. When you have a scenario in mind, answer the following prompts.

Describe the negative emotion or other painful experience:

_____
_____
_____
_____
_____
_____

SAYING THE *WRONG* THING

What were your internal experiences at the time? What were you imagining? Were you thinking about events that occurred in the past, or imagining things that might happen in the future?

_____
_____
_____
_____
_____
_____

What were your physiological experiences at the time? Were there any signs of a fight-flight-freeze-fawn reaction, such as a racing heart, restlessness, or muscle tension?

_____
_____
_____
_____
_____
_____

How did you act in response to these negative feelings? If you notice any responses that reflect fight, flight, freeze, or fawn, label those.

_____
_____
_____
_____
_____
_____

Chapter 6: *The Unintended Cost of Control*

Were there any societal messages influencing how you were thinking or reacting to your experiences? Do you notice any judgments or evaluations that might have been the result of toxic positivity or other ways society teaches us to treat our emotional experiences?

_____
_____
_____
_____
_____
_____

The Control Agenda in Conversation

As you've likely guessed, these same concepts also apply to difficult or challenging conversations. For example, when we are afraid of saying something hurtful or "wrong," or when we have strong reactions to what another person is saying, our instinct is often to fight against or avoid those potential threats. But once again, attempting to control the uncontrollable is often unhelpful at best, and potentially harmful in the end. Here are a few examples we have heard from colleagues, clients, friends, and family who have attempted to suppress or control their feelings to avoid saying the wrong thing:

- A mother is afraid of using her child's pronouns incorrectly and being perceived as a "bad parent," so she avoids using pronouns altogether.
- A psychologist "zones out" in a meeting during a discussion of race and diversity in the workplace because he is afraid that he will be reminded of his own history of trauma related to race and discrimination.
- A young adult client changes the subject every time her partner brings up the idea of having children because she is worried that her desire to prioritize her career will come across as selfish.
- A teacher notices that he is calling on students less often if their names are more difficult for him to pronounce.

You can probably think of your own examples of avoiding certain conversations or other means of escaping interpersonal discomfort. Does it work?

Molly's Story—The Cost of Saying Nothing

I completed my internship at one of the VA Health Care System sites. Part of my training involved leading group therapy for veterans alongside a supervisor. I recall stepping into the room on the first day of group and hearing inappropriate, sexist comments about my appearance. When I tuned into my internal experience, I noticed:

- **Physical sensations:** racing heart, shortened breath, sweaty hands, quavering voice, shaky limbs
- **Emotions:** anxiety, embarrassment, fear
- **Thoughts:** "It's my first session; I don't want to damage rapport right off the bat by saying something stupid." "I'm just a trainee; it's not my place to speak up." "My supervisor should say something." "Maybe I'm being overdramatic."

I was writhing in discomfort and highly motivated to escape from it. So, what did I do? I said nothing and continued to lead group as though nothing had happened. Problem solved, right? Wrong. I still felt painfully anxious, embarrassed, and fearful during the group session and long after it ended. But now, I also had the following:

- **Physical sensations:** nausea, sinking feeling
- **Emotions:** disgust, self-loathing, disappointment
- **Thoughts:** "Wow, how spineless are you? You knew what was happening was inappropriate, but you were too cowardly to do something about it."

As I consider the situation now, I imagine my supervisor also felt quite uncomfortable and didn't know what to say, so he didn't say anything either. His avoidance modeled to me that this was not a matter worth speaking up about and perhaps made me even less inclined to do so in the future. My own avoidance also blocked the possibility of a kind, but corrective, learning opportunity for the group members to get feedback about how to interact more respectfully. Saying nothing implied that it was acceptable to behave that way. Lastly, there easily could have been other group members victimized by similar dynamics—people who would have benefited if my supervisor and I had demonstrated how to set appropriate boundaries. In short, much opportunity for learning and improved connection was lost.

Chapter 6: *The Unintended Cost of Control*

Exercise—What Are You Running From?

Now, we would like to invite *you* to utilize a brief mindfulness practice to consider a specific time when you were concerned about saying the wrong thing, or when you had another fear related to a difficult conversation. You may read or follow along using this link so you can fully engage without distraction: www.sayingthewrongthing.com/audio/control-agenda.

Start by finding a comfortable but alert position. Allow your feet or body to ground into the earth, with your hands resting gently by your sides or in your lap. Close your eyes or fix your gaze softly in front of you. Take these first few moments to breathe deeply at your own pace.

Now, recall a time when you were very concerned that you might say the wrong thing. Take your time in recalling details as fully as you can: Where were you? What did the space look like? Do you recall what you could see, hear, smell, and feel around you in this moment? Consider the context as well: What was happening in this interaction? Who were you with? What exactly was said?

Now think back to your internal experience at the time: How were you feeling? What physical sensations were showing up in your body? Butterflies in your stomach, a lump in your throat, or tension in your neck, shoulders, or fists? What was showing up for you as you considered whether to say something?

What emotions were present? Anxiety? Fear? Anger? Sadness? Excitement? Take a moment to get clear on what you were feeling. How intense were these emotions at the time? Mild? Strong? Somewhere in between?

What thoughts were running through your mind as you watched this interaction unfold or participated in the conversation? Were you having judgments about what you should or shouldn't say? Having thoughts about the other person? Thoughts about your true feelings? About what would happen if you expressed yourself? What are all the uncomfortable elements you wanted to get away from?

Now take a moment to return to the natural rhythm of your breath. Release the image of this memory as you ground yourself again in the present moment. Observe how you are feeling—even now—in response to something that has long passed. Whenever you're ready, gently open your eyes and return to this space.

SAYING THE *WRONG* THING

How was that for you? Take a moment to reflect on what showed up. What distressing thoughts, feelings, and physical sensations came up for you when you were presented with the possibility of saying the wrong thing?

_____
_____
_____

Here are some common responses that have showed up for clients and participants who've completed our workshop.

Physical Sensations	Emotions	Thoughts
• Heart racing	• Anxiety	• "What does it matter what I say?"
• Nausea	• Fear	• "Is it my place?"
• Sweating	• Uncertainty	• "I don't want to upset them." / "They're going to be upset at me." / "I will lose friends."
• Shallow breathing	• Insecurity	
• Fidgeting	• Panic	• "I'm incompetent / not smart enough / not the expert here / inadequate / not made for this."
• Lack of eye contact	• Irritability	
• Difficulty concentrating	• Embarrassment	• "They will get mad at / won't like / will judge / will reject me."
	• Guilt	
• Muscle tension	• Doubt	• "It will be hurtful."
• Restlessness	• Rejection	• "I will be imposing my values on them."
• Numbness	• Shame	• "It's not safe."
• Redness/flushing	• Confusion	• "I will be punished."
• Fatigue	• Burnout	• "I want to be nice."
• Heartburn	• Depletion	• "I can't be bothered to have this fight right now."
• Trembling voice	• Apprehension	
• Clamminess	• Resignation	• "I will make things worse."
• Twitchiness	• Hesitation	• "I will be invalidated."
• Chills	• Uneasiness	• "I'm wrong."
• Heaviness	• Vulnerability	• "They know better."
	• Desperation	• "This isn't the right forum for this."
	• Overwhelm	• "People will think I'm bad."
	• Irritability	• "It will create distance between me and the client."
	• Dread	• "Are they allowed to have their thoughts?"

Chapter 6: *The Unintended Cost of Control*

Next, take some time to think of the strategies you've used to avoid or suppress these thoughts, sensations, and feelings. What have you done to avoid saying the wrong thing? Consider the situation you identified during your mindfulness practice. What did you say (or not say)? What did you do (or not do)? List as many as you can think of.

_____
_____
_____
_____
_____

It can be interesting and difficult to think about avoidance techniques. There are so many, and they can be very insidious! Here are some common ones that people use.

In-the-Moment Avoidance Techniques	Before-or-After Avoidance Techniques
• **Say nothing:** The freeze response activates, and you become immobilized, remaining silent despite a tumult of thoughts and feelings. • **Redirect:** You hear a comment and choose to change the subject. • **Agree/placate/validate:** You look to find the kernel of truth or play devil's advocate, even around issues you are passionately in opposition to. • **Smile/laugh/joke:** You nervously smile, laugh, nod vigorously, or otherwise nonverbally communicate agreement or acceptance. • **Spout facts/overexplain:** You launch into teacher mode, providing facts, context, and education. • **Check out:** You dissociate and go to your "mental place happy break," as one workshop attendant called it.	• **Procrastinate:** You put off an important conversation, as it is always "not the right time" to broach the issue. • **Isolate:** You avoid being around those who might invoke anxiety, even if they matter to you. • **Use substances:** You drink alcohol or use drugs to dull discomfort from past or impending conversations. • **Work harder:** You dive into the literature in desperate attempts to become the "expert" on difficult topics. Surely you will never be caught unprepared again! • **Overprepare:** You rehearse the perfect response ad nauseam. This strategy works so long as everyone adheres to the script—speaking and reacting exactly as you expect them to.

SAYING THE *WRONG* THING

As you can see, these strategies to get away from discomfort are universal. We engage in them for a reason. For most of us, there is short-term gratification: We get to delay anxiety and feel momentary reprieve. But does it work in the long term? And is there a cost?

> ### Steph's Story—The Hardest Conversation
>
> I am a pediatric psychologist who works in a children's hospital with sick and dying children. On the pediatric floor, they sometimes give toddlers mini "shopping carts" so they can walk around the hospital with their caregivers while being less of a fall risk. Once, I was walking with a medical resident when we came across an adorable toddler—bald and slightly bloated from chemotherapy, steroids, and other treatments—pushing one of these tiny shopping carts. I turned to the resident and said, "So cute! And *this* is why I work in pediatrics versus adults!" The resident responded, "This is why I could *never* work in pediatrics. It's impossible not to feel empathy for your patients."
>
> I firmly believe that empathy and perspective-taking make for better providers. But as the resident pointed out, empathy can also make things harder. Doctors enter medicine to heal—not to feel helpless in the context of untreatable terminal disease. Their empathy toward patients and families can lead them to understandably avoid sad conversations about death and dying. Unfortunately, avoiding hard conversations can come at a cost. It can lead to prolonged suffering; treatments with adverse effects and no chance of success; patients who have been denied a voice in end-of-life choices; or patients and families who have been presented with conflicting messages about curative versus palliative interventions that exacerbate distress.
>
> For example, I once worked with a seventeen-year-old patient with terminal brain cancer. Providers knew from the beginning that this cancer had a low likelihood of being cured and relayed this to the parents—but not to the patient, because of how difficult the conversation would be and the complications of procuring parental permission. When I began working with the patient, he shared that he was worried the treatment was ineffective and was confused about the optimistic messages he was receiving. He wanted to know about his treatment and prognosis, even if it was bad news. He wanted to have a say in his care.
>
> When I shared this with the parents, they agreed that he should have a voice in his remaining care but struggled with how to have this discussion with their child. They worried that if they acknowledged out loud, "Our child is dying," his death would imminently occur, which is a common and understandable fear held by families. The parents did consent that we disclose the truth to their son, but the medical team's

Chapter 6: *The Unintended Cost of Control*

> own avoidance meant more delays in having the conversation. Ultimately, he was discharged home to hospice without having the opportunity to voice his preferences or address the existential questions of his mortal circumstance while in the hospital with his treating team.
>
> Providers (and all humans) struggle with accepting that death is imminent. But death is a part of life, and families deserve to have providers willing to face the inevitable with them. In this case, the patient was willing to bravely confront the uncomfortable even when the adults in his life were not.

Exercise—The Consequences

Think back to the difficult conversation you identified in the *What Are You Running From?* exercise. Did you experience any negative consequences when you avoided saying the wrong thing? How did you feel about yourself after the incident? What new emotions, thoughts, and physical sensations arose as a result? What happened to the original thoughts, feelings, and sensations?

_____
_____
_____
_____
_____
_____

SAYING THE *WRONG* THING

When we've asked our clients and workshop participants to describe the negative consequences they've experienced as a result of avoidance, here are the common responses.

Physical Sensations	Emotions	Thoughts
• Exhaustion • Nausea • Restlessness • Dissociation • Muscle tension • Poor sleep • Stomachache • Low energy • Lack of appetite • Sweatiness • Weakness • Inability to relax	• Sadness • Frustration • Remorse • Shame • Irritability • Disconnection • Guilt • Self-criticism • Disingenuousness • Stress • Resentment • Hopelessness • Regret • Loneliness	• "Silence is violence. I am part of the problem." • "I didn't learn anything." • "The problem escalated." • "I perpetuated injustice." • "They didn't learn anything." • "People felt unsupported by me." • "I'm damaged." • "I missed out on a meaningful connection." • "I reinforced the status quo." • "Nothing changes." • "I was selfish not to address it."

This is the ironic effect of the control agenda: When you attempt to avoid distress, you end up amplifying the very distress you are trying to prevent and experiencing other unwanted and uncomfortable thoughts, feelings, and sensations. After all, when you act in a way that violates your values, it can lead to a sense of disingenuousness.

So, if you cannot control your emotions, thoughts, and body sensations, what are you supposed to do when things get uncomfortable? We're very glad you asked! The answer is *acceptance*, which will be the focus of our next chapter.

Chapter 6: *The Unintended Cost of Control*

Play and Practice

- Choose a word or simple phrase, ideally something that is not important to you or emotionally charged in any way. Write that word here: _____. Now, try *not* to think of that word or phrase for twenty-four hours. Keep a tally of the number of times it comes up (including dreams!). After the twenty-four hours are over, jot down any reflections you have on what strategies you tried, which were effective, and anything else about the activity you found interesting.

- The next time you have a difficult conversation, use the following *Control Agenda Detective* template to reflect on how the experience went. What did you hope to get out of the conversation? What strategies did you use to achieve this goal? Did they work? The key is to engage in this activity *after* the conversation occurs. No need to plan or do anything differently than you normally would in the moment.

- Role-play a difficult conversation with a trusted person, setting a timer to go off every sixty seconds for five minutes (or longer if you choose). Each time the timer goes off, use the *Mindfulness in Conversation* template to note the physical sensations, emotions, and thoughts that are coming up for you. If your partner is also engaging in the exercise, debrief afterward, noticing similarities and differences across your experiences.

Takeaway Points

- There are biological and social factors that predispose humans to use avoidance and control in the face of danger. Because of our incredible ability to think and imagine, we tend to overuse these strategies in the face of imagined threats.

- Unfortunately, attempts to control or avoid thoughts, feelings, and sensations have proven to be both ineffective and damaging.

- When it comes to challenging conversations, particularly those that matter to you, the stakes can feel high, and your instinct to avoid perceived danger can be especially strong. There are personal and interpersonal costs to ineffective control strategies in this context.

Control Agenda Detective

This activity can follow any challenging conversation you find yourself in. If you are not having any difficult discussions (lucky you!), you can also role-play a challenging conversation with a partner to simulate the activity.

1. Describe the conversation in the space here.

   _____
   _____
   _____
   _____
   _____

2. What did you want to get out of the conversation? Include your ideal outcome but also any smaller goals, such as staying calm or getting your point across. Did you have any long-term goals, such as maintaining a relationship or making a lasting change?

   _____
   _____
   _____
   _____
   _____

3. What strategies did you use to try to accomplish these outcomes? Notice which strategies were in the service of control or avoidance.

   _____
   _____
   _____
   _____
   _____

4. Did your strategies work? Did they help accomplish the goals you listed in question 2? Did they come with any costs or consequences? Were they more successful with one type of goal versus another (e.g., short-term versus long-term)?

_____
_____
_____
_____
_____

5. Was the approach you took to this conversation similar to or different from your typical approach to difficult conversations? Reflect on whether your answers are common patterns for you or unique to this conversation.

_____
_____
_____
_____
_____

Mindfulness in Conversation

Topic of conversation: _____

Minute	Physical Sensations	Thoughts	Emotions
1			
2			
3			
4			
5			

ped
PART THREE

Your Road Map for Talking About What Matters

CHAPTER 7

Making Space for What Shows Up

> *"You couldn't relive your life, skipping the awful parts, without losing what made it worthwhile. You had to accept it as a whole—like the world, or the person you loved."*
>
> —Stewart O'Nan

What Is Acceptance?

As we mentioned at the end of the last chapter, acceptance is the antidote to avoidance and control. This may be a hard pill to swallow, especially if you have negative reactions to the word *acceptance*. So often, people believe that acceptance carries implications of powerlessness, complacency, or even collusion in the face of difficulty. But acceptance is none of those things. Rather, acceptance involves a willingness to experience the difficult emotions that are an inherent part of being human, rather than trying to fight against these experiences in futility. When you practice acceptance, you free up energy to act in ways that are consistent with your values. Acceptance provides you with a chance to impart change for yourself and others.

Let us illustrate with an example: You are driving in traffic and someone cuts you off, racing to get ahead and startling you in the process. Nonacceptance might look like this: "What the hell?! You jerk! How dare you! I'll show you . . ." When you lean into thoughts like this, you may notice a rise in blood pressure, rapid breathing, erratic driving, or even attempts to catch up to the person and "pay them back" for their transgression. At best, this can lead to lasting feelings of adrenaline, anger, or righteousness that may continue to impact your attitude throughout the day. At worst, you might put yourself or others at risk by invoking dangerous levels of road rage. Is it worth it?

In contrast, if you were to use acceptance in this situation, you would acknowledge the pang of anxiety and anger that you experience after being cut off. You would then take a few deep breaths and acknowledge that while the person's actions were frustrating, frightening, and potentially harmful, there may be innumerable reasons for their behavior. They might be late for a job interview that means the difference between providing for their family or struggling through another month of food and shelter insecurity. They may, having received terrible news that a loved one is in the hospital, be rushing to be by their side. They may be experiencing debilitating physical symptoms and need to get off the road immediately to avoid further harm or damage.

And sure, they might just be a jerk. The reason doesn't actually matter. You get to choose your behavior anyway. By having the willingness to experience your frustration and fear without acting impulsively on them, you create the space to make a choice: You can get riled up, chase this person down, and make them pay. Or you can take a deep breath, let it go, and move on with the things in your life that are important to you.

As this example illustrates, acceptance is allowing reality to be as it is so you can see and respond clearly and effectively. Acceptance is not saying that a difficult situation is permissible or okay. It is not giving up or tolerating unacceptable behavior. Acceptance is a conscious choice to allow *your* thoughts, feelings, and sensations to be present as they are, without engaging in the control agenda. In doing so, you can redirect that energy toward your values. For this reason, we often prefer the term *willingness* instead of *acceptance* and use them interchangeably.

A Word on Denial

You may have some familiarity with the five stages of grief as described by Elisabeth Kübler-Ross (1997): denial, anger, bargaining, depression, and acceptance. Although these stages are not linear, denial is often one of the first people experience in the wake of a loss, tragedy, or otherwise unimaginable circumstances. On the surface, denial is the antithesis

Chapter 7: Making Space for What Shows Up

of acceptance. However, it is often a necessary and functional stage to experience for a short while because it can be a protective mechanism against horror or overwhelm. Most people understand the reality of a loss, trauma, or act of wrongdoing on a cognitive level, but it may be difficult for them to fully integrate it into their experience, especially when the loss is sudden or unexpected. During this phase, the body and mind may postpone "accepting reality" so the affected individual can simply survive the situation and move through day-to-day tasks. This is not to be rushed or downplayed, and in time, most people will naturally move through the other phases of grief. In other words, denial is a place to visit, but not to live.

However, becoming *stuck* in denial can cause significant problems. Consider someone who refuses to accept that a loved one has passed, insisting that they are still here and will be back any day now. This can hinder the natural healing process that allows this person to move forward and continue to live fully within reality. Or consider someone who denies the realities of racism, the horrors of the Holocaust, the ravages of climate change, or other corrosive and ongoing tragedies. While it may be protective to keep their head in the sand about issues that are overwhelming or that call for inconvenient or uncomfortable lifestyle changes, there are serious short- and long-term repercussions for not responding to crises as they are. Furthermore, denial—or *unwillingness*, as we like to call it—requires a tremendous amount of physical and psychic energy to maintain, as illustrated in the following exercise.

Exercise—Unwillingness Versus Willingness

For this exercise, you may read along, pausing for several moments between each paragraph, or follow along using this link so you can fully engage without distraction: www.sayingthewrongthing.com/audio/willingness.

Take a moment to find a comfortable, alert position for this exercise. Allow the body to settle and your eyes to close, if you're willing. Or if you'd rather, find a place a few feet in front of you to softly fix your gaze. Begin to breathe deeply and at your own pace. No need to force or shape the breath in any way.

Begin to observe the sensations you feel in and on your body. These might include where your body contacts the surface you're sitting or lying on. Notice whether the surface feels hard or soft, smooth or varied. Notice the feel of any fabric or other textile sensations on your skin. What are the temperatures of the various surfaces or areas around your body? How are they the same or different? What sensations feel neutral or pleasant? What sensations feel somewhat unpleasant? Perhaps you notice some mild pain or discomfort in your body, like a tense muscle, an itch, or an urge to sneeze. Focus on this mildly unpleasant sensation—on this sensation that you would prefer not be there.

Now, we invite you to actively practice being unwilling to have that unpleasant sensation. Fight against it internally, deny its existence, try to make it stop however you can. Notice what happens as you do this. What happens within your body? To your breath? What thoughts do you have to rehearse to yourself to push this sensation away? What emotions begin to surface as you fight against this sensation? What happens to the sensation you wish to banish? Observe with curiosity.

Now, let go of unwillingness. Allow that unwanted sensation to be exactly as it is; perhaps even invite it like a guest into your home. Relax into it. Breathe into it. Hold it gently. What happens in your body as you practice accepting this unpleasant reality? What is the pace and tenor of your thoughts as you allow it to be with you? How do you feel emotionally when you drop the struggle and practice willingness to be with what is?

Take these last few moments to return to your breath, focusing your attention on the steady inhale and exhale of each breath. Begin to envision where you are seated in the room. And when you're ready, allow your eyes to gently open, if they've been closed, and return to this space.

What sensation did you choose and why?

_____
_____
_____
_____

What happened when you were unwilling to experience this sensation as it is? Did the sensation go away? Did any other thoughts, emotions, or sensations arise in response?

_____
_____
_____
_____

Chapter 7: *Making Space for What Shows Up*

What happened when you embodied willingness and acceptance? Did the sensation go away? How did you feel?

_____
_____
_____
_____

> ### Danielle's Story—The Cost of Unwillingness
>
> Early in the COVID-19 pandemic, I had a lot of fear for my family. I had recently moved to Oregon while my family remained in Louisiana; I felt worried about their safety, the misinformation they may have been getting, and the fact that I couldn't be with them if something were to happen. In an attempt to alleviate my worries, I constantly sought reassurance when I talked to them on the phone. I asked about their well-being and scrutinized all the behaviors they were engaging in. I tried to convince them to do things differently than everyone around them, but this did nothing to assuage my worry. Instead, it usually ended in an argument and resulted in the bonus thoughts that I was a "bad daughter" and a "bad sister." At one point, I resorted to the even worse strategy of avoiding talking to my family altogether. So, if you're keeping count, I started with one painful experience—worry—and to get rid of it, I added "bad daughter," "bad sister," family conflict, and isolation on top of it. And guess what—I was still worried.

Why Bother with Willingness?

Being willing to sit with discomfort is difficult, to say the least. And when it comes to things that are important to you, it can be downright agonizing. Why would you subject yourself to this burden? Well, it turns out there are several reasons!

1. Avoidance strategies don't work and can even make things worse.
2. Acceptance and willingness *do* work.
3. This may be a little hard to believe, but there are useful things hidden in your discomfort. Yes, it's true!

SAYING THE *WRONG* THING

Let's expand upon the research behind these three reasons. First, as discussed in the previous chapter and illustrated in Danielle's preceding example, avoidance strategies don't work and often result in even more physiological and emotional distress. In fact, research has found that avoidance can lead to depression, anxiety, obsessive-compulsive behaviors, and posttraumatic stress symptoms (Akbari et al., 2022). Importantly, it can also interfere with your ability to form strong interpersonal relationships (Gerhart et al., 2014) and can contribute to feelings of social isolation and loneliness (Maitland et al., 2020).

Second, research has found that when people practice acceptance in the face of difficulty, they experience more positive mental health outcomes (Nakamura & Orth, 2005). For example, not only can acceptance buffer the effects of posttraumatic stress (Jung & Kim, 2020), but it also lowers the risk of suicidal ideation (Moscardini et al., 2024). In short, people recover more quickly from adversity by accepting reality as it is rather than refusing to acknowledge it. And much like the other skills we are teaching you, acceptance is a skill you can learn and strengthen. By doing so, you will regain precious time and energy previously spent on ineffective control strategies. Better start thinking of all the things you would like to do instead!

Third, there are usually things we *want* hiding within our discomfort. That may be hard to believe, but hear us out! Remember our discussion about the control agenda in the previous chapter? Uncomfortable experiences like loss, grief, and suffering represent only one side of a coin. These sources of discomfort wouldn't exist or matter without the other side: joy, happiness, and value in the people and experiences in our lives. That means the depths of our struggles are often a direct reflection of the depth of our values.

Think of a recent experience in your own life that brought with it challenging feelings, self-criticism, or physical or emotional pain. Peel back the layers of that pain and look at who or what was the source of that difficult experience. Was there a person you cared about at the center of this conflict? Something you wanted or thought would bring your life meaning? Something you needed that was taken away or held just out of reach?

_____
_____
_____
_____
_____

Chapter 7: *Making Space for What Shows Up*

What did you notice? The very nature of grief is the loss of someone or something that we cared deeply for. Although we can attempt to avoid these feelings of loss or disappointment by becoming apathetic, nihilistic, isolated, and noncommittal, that comes at the cost of brilliant experiences like love, connection, and passion. Is that worth it?

To further illustrate our point, think back to the 2023 hit film *Barbie*, where the title character is given an opportunity to remain in the contrived but perfect and predictable Barbieland forever or become human. Before making this decision, she is reminded of the totality of the human experience: sexism, racism, war, death, grief, loss . . . *and* family, friendship, love, nature, adventure, wonder, excitement, choice. Barbie contemplates these questions and choices that we are all privileged and burdened by, ultimately making the decision to embrace her humanity and the imperfections that come with it. Like Barbie, we all face choices like this, but on a much more frequent basis. Day to day and even moment to moment, we are faced with a choice between turning toward the things that are important to us or turning away from the pains of humanity.

But What Does Willingness Really Look Like?

If you're nodding along and agreeing with this chapter but still finding yourself scratching your head about what acceptance or willingness actually means, you're not alone. We've heard from countless clients and workshop participants (and even each other!) that it can be hard to put a finger on exactly what these concepts look like in practice—not to mention that we are so well-versed at avoidance, many of us have little experience in consciously doing the opposite. So, what exactly does willingness look like?

Willingness is a values-based *choice* to allow discomfort to exist. "Values-based" means that the choice is made in service of something that matters to you. And by choice, we do not mean a one-time decision that, once made, is final and everlasting. Rather, willingness involves an ongoing, moment-to-moment decision to choose whether discomfort can remain, in the service of your values. To make this type of choice, you must be aware of the discomfort *and* clear on your values, which is why you learned about those two skills first. It may take practice to recognize when you are choosing to allow discomfort, but over time, it will get easier to identify moments of willingness and acceptance.

To illustrate this concept more concretely, see if you're *willing* (see what we did there?) to hold a piece of ice in your hand. Notice how long you are willing to hold it for no other reason than because we are asking you to. Take note of how long you held it, just to humor us: _____.

Now, think about someone you care about. What is something you hope for that person? Imagine that the longer you hold an ice cube, the more you give this person what you hope for them. Take a second piece of ice in your other hand and hold it as long as you can with this person in mind. How long did you hold the second piece of ice? Take note of the time here: _____.

We're guessing your answers are a bit different. Each moment of holding on to the ice cube in service of the person you were thinking about was a moment of willingness. Take note of what that felt like and reflect on any additional observations below.

_____
_____
_____
_____
_____
_____

Are You *Willing* to Say the Wrong Thing?

Initiating a difficult conversation requires tremendous courage for a few reasons. First, you must be willing to endure the uncertainty of what may come with no real promise that you will get your desired outcome. Second, you must be willing to allow the other person's thoughts and feelings to be present. After all, when you broach challenging topics with people who hold different views from your own, you must be open to *their* unique set of life experiences, fears, joys, and reactions that may be invoked during the discussion—not just your own. This is an added layer of acceptance that we refer to as *interpersonal willingness*, and it is vulnerable territory to enter with anyone. What's more, the stakes may change based on the type of relationship and the power differentials at play (e.g., talking with a partner, parent, teacher, or supervisor). How can you be aware and respectful of your and others' internal experiences without bulldozing one another?

Chapter 7: *Making Space for What Shows Up*

As therapist and boundaries coach Molly Davis (2024) says, you must honor the self *and* honor others. While you are allowed to think and feel all sorts of things, how you act must not cause harm or disrespect to others. The same goes for the other person in the conversation. In a boundaried relationship, you can kindly express when a line has been crossed or describe what you need in order to be willing to continue the discussion. (This reflects the foundational skill of radical candor you learned in chapter 3!) You must also be open to feedback whenever you inadvertently (and invariably) cross boundaries into someone else's rights for respect and autonomy. All of us are susceptible to saying the wrong thing, particularly when discussing what matters most. Being able to bravely and willingly enter those spaces involves knowing that you will make mistakes, learning how to take space, and making repairs when needed. As with all things, it takes practice.

Annette's Story—A Child with a Kind Heart

I have been a people-pleaser most of my life, and I am pretty good at it! There really is nothing like the feeling that my actions may have resulted in another person's happiness. This disposition has taught me many skills throughout my life, as I am good at keeping the peace, understanding others' perspectives, and losing myself in others' experiences of joy. However, underneath those benefits lies a gnawing sense of insecurity. I feel the need to seek the reassurance that, yes, I am a *good person*. As a result, I often find myself prioritizing the needs and wants of others so I can ultimately avoid conflict and keep the peace.

For example, I have navigated one intimate relationship after another where I was taken advantage of and manipulated. I was missing a solid grasp of what I wanted in these relationships because I was so used to putting my needs and wants aside for others, yet I simply did not have the skills to do any differently. When I started acknowledging these people-pleaser qualities as neither good nor bad but relics of a child with a kind heart—one who was just being a human with other imperfect humans—I was able to accept my people-pleasing qualities while also learning new skills and setting new boundaries to improve my relationships. This was and still is a variable process; I notice myself making progress, then regressing, noticing those ingrained behaviors, picking back up, growing from that, and so on. I can still see these tendencies, but instead of spiraling into self-doubt and shame, I can be compassionate and patient with myself. And with progress, there have also been surprises.

Once I moved toward acceptance, I began experiencing new emotions, specifically anger. I realized that when I had been avoiding conflict, I had been avoiding the opportunity to practice advocating for myself. Now that I was speaking up for myself, I placed blame on others, name-called, made unfair assumptions, and generally surprised myself with how little control I had when I was upset. With practice and support, I eventually became accustomed to the sensations of anger. I recognized that anger is my body's way of telling me that I'm not feeling great. And that's okay. It's okay to be human. I have learned how to manage angry feelings in a less clumsy and more skillful way. Learning how to express my boundaries has been difficult, but practicing acceptance has opened the door to being more compassionate with myself. And life is a lot better with these new boundaries, thankfully. It's still hard to be human sometimes, but better to be alive.

Chapter 7: *Making Space for What Shows Up*

As Annette's story illustrates, interpersonal willingness has its own unique challenges, and it can be easy to fall into patterns of avoidance when it comes to interacting with others. Have you ever noticed that you were overly concerned with making sure other people were not experiencing negative emotions? Or, conversely, wondered why others did not share in the negative emotions you were experiencing? Maybe you've looked around after some instance of injustice and thought, *Why is no one else reacting as angrily as I am?* Or perhaps you've noticed that in group situations, you tend to be the one keeping the peace, ensuring other people enjoy themselves and explaining people's actions so that no one feels offended. As if our own thoughts and emotions aren't enough to deal with!

In challenging conversations, you may notice the instinct to control and avoid not only your own feelings, but also those of the other person. This raises the difficulty level on willingness so you can remain in touch with your values and objectives, and it can be especially difficult to do in real time. However, there are things you can do to prepare in advance. The first step is familiarizing yourself with the difficult thoughts, feelings, and sensations that may come up during the conversation so that you can acknowledge these without as strong a compulsion to do anything about them. The following exercise is intended to help you with this.

Exercise—Uninvited Meeting Guests

This exercise will help you envision the difficult thoughts, feelings, and sensations that might come during a challenging conversation. Instead of fighting against these experiences, you will practice acknowledging, labeling, and making space for them. To begin, imagine that you'll be having a tough conversation in a meeting space where other people might show up—but in this case, the other "meeting guests" will be the thoughts and feelings that come up during the conversation. If you are someone who spends a lot of time in virtual meetings, it can be fun to picture these meeting guests as squares on a screen. Alternatively, people at an in-person meeting or any other group event you can think of will work (e.g., a house party, a Sunday dinner, a school meeting).

1. Look back to chapter 1 and the list of challenging topics you identified as being a priority. For example, perhaps you want to talk to your boss about more flexible

SAYING THE *WRONG* THING

work hours, or to a family member about a big decision you've made. Briefly describe the topic here.

_____

_____

_____

_____

2. Once you have chosen the conversation, doodle the two of you talking in your meeting venue in the space below—no artistic skills required!

3. If you could speak your mind to this person fully and without fear, what would you like to say to them? Use a speech bubble to add this to your drawing, like the one shown to the right.

I'd like a raise.

Chapter 7: *Making Space for What Shows Up*

4. When you imagine saying this, what emotions arise? What thoughts go through your mind? What sensations do you feel in your body? These are your uninvited guests. Write these aspects of your internal experience on your side of the drawing. You can simply write the words or get elaborate and draw them as actual meeting guests. For example, maybe your fear is a nervous guest who stays in the corner the whole time, while your thought *I don't deserve this* is a loud guest who interrupts all the time.

5. What do you think the other person might be feeling, thinking, and sensing during this conversation? Write these things down on their side of the drawing, either as words or as more elaborate meeting guests.

6. Reflect on the crowd that has assembled in your meeting. What would happen if you allowed these guests to stay and do as they please while you finish your conversation?

_____
_____
_____
_____

As this exercise illustrates, our thoughts and feelings can be a distraction, and becoming familiar with them ahead of time will diminish their power. Other strategies that can be used include clarifying your objectives for the conversation and calming your nervous system so that you have extra resources to accept what comes up. If you find yourself overwhelmed or ruminating before or after a difficult conversation, you can try practicing mindful breathing (see the *Square Breathing* exercise in chapter 4), doing progressive muscle relaxation (sequentially tensing and then relaxing different muscle groups from head to toe; visit www.sayingthewrongthing.com/audio/pmr for a guided exercise), going on a brisk walk or run, or even splashing cool water on your face. All these strategies will provide more space and clarity on what you want to accomplish and who you want to be in the conversation.

Having familiarized yourself with the thoughts and feelings likely to arise, clarified your values, and connected with the present moment, you will be well prepared (and, ideally, willing) to have an effective conversation. Willingness is a skill that improves over time, and there will be ups and downs no matter how skilled you are. Make sure you aren't setting unreasonable expectations for yourself, and remember that placing judgment on moments of unwillingness is neither reasonable nor helpful. You will have moments of avoidance, and that's okay. Every moment of willingness is a success, and even simply noticing avoidance can be hugely beneficial to your long-term growth. When you do have moments of avoidance or attempts at control, you can reflect on those after the fact to strengthen your skills even further.

It's also important to recognize when willingness is not the solution—when the time is not right for a particular conversation. For example, if you find that your emotions (or the other person's) are escalating faster than you'd like, you can always press pause and take a break. This might look like saying, "I'm starting to feel a little frustrated and think we should table this conversation until I can respond more calmly." It is important that if you take a time-out from a conversation, you have a clear plan to time back in: "Let's plan to revisit this tomorrow morning over breakfast. Does that work for you?" Without a plan to return to a conversation, this strategy can turn into avoidance. Everything in perspective!

Finally, if you're finding it hard to tell whether leaving a conversation is effective or avoidant, you're in good company. It's not always an easy answer. The best thing you can do is revisit your values—holding your personal compass in your mind—and choose based on what seems most values-consistent. It's why we made sure to have the chapter on values come before this one, to guide you. We also think it will be helpful to figure out where you are most likely to get stuck. Identifying the areas that you tend to get hung up on will make identifying avoidance even easier. And that's exactly what we'll turn to in the next chapter.

Chapter 7: *Making Space for What Shows Up*

Play and Practice

- Make a list of all the conversations or topics in which you've worried about saying the wrong thing, actually said the wrong thing, or seen someone else say the wrong thing. List the body sensations, thoughts, and emotions that tend to come up for you when tasked with conversations like these.

- Pair up with someone you trust and have a conversation about a difficult topic. Each person should choose one topic that they are uncomfortable or unfamiliar with to explore. Describe the experiences that come up for you both with openness and accuracy. Take fifteen minutes each before switching. At the close of the practice, share what it was like to enter a brave space together, despite any judgments or fears that showed up.

- Write about a time when you successfully engaged in a difficult conversation even though you were worried about saying or doing the wrong thing. What made that possible? How can you replicate this experience?

- Think of someone who is skilled at giving and receiving difficult feedback. Call them and ask them to walk you through how they prepare for difficult conversations. How do they accept and manage the discomfort they feel?

Takeaway Points

- The alternative to avoidance is acceptance, which involves acknowledging the reality of a situation instead of resisting it.

- Acceptance is *not* the same thing as resigning yourself to something you don't want, tolerating unacceptable behavior, or saying things are "okay" when they aren't.

- Another word for acceptance is willingness, which involves making a moment-to-moment choice to allow discomfort in the service of values.

- Interpersonal willingness involves opening yourself up to your own discomfort as well as the discomfort of others that a hard conversation might engender.

- Becoming acquainted and compassionate with your distress will allow you to move forward in a more values-consistent way.

CHAPTER 8

Putting Things into Perspective

> "There is nothing new under the sun, but there are new suns."
> —Octavia E. Butler

By now, you have learned that trying to control or avoid unwanted thoughts, emotions, and sensations is both ineffective and problematic, and that the alternative is to consciously allow those experiences to exist. Easier said than done, we know. But while you can't control your internal experiences, there is something you can do to make accepting them less difficult: You can change your *relationship* with them.

This chapter covers two key ACT skills that are intertwined and will help you do just that. The first is **cognitive defusion**, or getting healthy distance from your thoughts and experiences. The second is **perspective-taking**, or seeing thoughts and experiences from multiple vantage points. Together, these skills can help you change your relationship to difficult thoughts and feelings that might otherwise stand in the way of productive, meaningful conversations.

Creating Distance with Cognitive Defusion

Before diving into cognitive *defusion*, let's take a moment to look at the inflexible side of the spectrum, or cognitive *fusion*. What does your mind tell you when you read "two plus two equals _____"? Write or draw your answer in the space on the following page.

SAYING THE *WRONG* THING

Did your mind say "four"? We might even consider that an "objectively true fact." If I have two marbles and you have two marbles and we put them together, we will see four marbles right there in front of our eyes.

Now, let's try another one. What does your mind tell you when you read "giraffe plus cat equals _____"? Write or draw your answer in the space below.

Chapter 8: *Putting Things into Perspective*

What did you imagine? Did you imagine a cat with a very long neck? A giraffe with whiskers? A very small giraffe or very big cat? A terrifying Frankenstein's-monster-like giraffecat? Whatever your mind came up with, we can agree it is not "objectively true," and probably not something you've ever imagined before (unless you are an animal-combining enthusiast—in which case, we love that for you!). And yet, it is so easy for our minds to imagine new and completely fantastical things. Terrifying giraffecats aside, we have many other thoughts that we simply accept as true and too often end up getting attached to. When we get stuck on thoughts, feelings, or other experiences, we call that **cognitive fusion**.

When two things are fused, they are combined, blended, or even melted together. Fusion cooking, for example, combines two or more culinary traditions to create new and unique flavors and cuisine. Glass fusing is an art form that uses heat to soften pieces of glass and join them together to make ornaments and other pieces. Both are examples of positive outcomes of merging separate things. However, being fused together sometimes means being *stuck* together, which denotes a lack of choice and may not be so positive. Think of a plastic container that forever holds the color and smell of food left inside a little too long. Or an unassuming moth stuck on one of those sticky fly papers (from the moth's perspective, not positive!). When we talk about cognitive fusion, we are referring to being *stuck* on our thoughts, feelings, or other experiences in an unhelpful way. You may be raising an eyebrow and wondering what it means to be stuck on a thought. Glad you asked!

Take a moment and say the following phrase in your mind: *The sky is blue*. Did you have any reactions to this thought? Putting aside any obscure memories of debating this question, this thought might appear to be objectively true. You might feel confident in its accuracy, and you likely do not feel negative about it appearing in your mind. Now, let's try another one. Take a moment and say the following phrase in your mind: *I do not need oxygen to live*. Did you have any reactions to this thought? Do you feel confident in the inaccuracy of the thought? Or perhaps you imagined yourself as a sea creature for whom it might be true. For most of us, a thought like this is easy to dismiss and move on with our day.

Now, let's examine one final thought. Take a moment to say the following phrase in your mind: *I'm not good enough*. Did you have any reactions to this thought? Did this thought feel familiar or unfamiliar? Did you notice whether your mind tried to label it as accurate or inaccurate? Did you notice any emotions or sensations arise in response to this thought? Did any memories, experiences, or even worries come up? Do you feel positive, negative, or neutral about having this thought in your mind? Maybe you're upset at us for even asking you to think it. Or maybe you're relieved that we used this example instead of *another* thought that gets in your way (perhaps something like *I'm unlovable, not smart enough, an impostor, a burden, a failure, broken . . .*).

When we have a strong reaction to or spend too much energy managing a thought, these are signs that we are stuck, or fused, to it. And this stuckness can cause problems in our lives. For example, imagine a person who is fused with the thought *I'm not smart enough*. If they believe this to be true, they may give up on goals that feel unattainable when this thought arises. Or they may spend all their energy trying to combat it by seeking higher degrees, even if their passions do not require advanced education. If being "smart" is an important family value, this thought could lead to significant depression. If this person perceives their friends and family as smarter and more capable, they may isolate themselves or endure interactions with severe anxiety about how they are being perceived.

In addition, we can be fused with positive thoughts just as easily as negative ones. For example, a person who is fused to the thought that they deserve a promotion at work may feel jealous or upset if a friend gets the promotion instead. Or consider a new graduate student who is accustomed to being at the top of their class and is fused with the thought of being "very intelligent." In graduate school, when they are suddenly surrounded by other high-achieving individuals, they may no longer be at the top of their class, causing sudden self-doubt. Similarly, a person who is fused with the belief that they are "exceptionally attractive" may experience panic and despair at any early signs of aging.

Now that we've covered the inflexibility of cognitive fusion, let's look at how we can use cognitive *de*fusion to more flexibly approach our thoughts and experiences. Think for a moment about how you feel when you hear the word *stupid*. What thoughts or feelings do you associate with this word? Are there any memories or fears associated with this word? Jot down what comes up for you when you hear it.

_____
_____
_____
_____

Chapter 8: *Putting Things into Perspective*

Now, think about how you feel when you hear the word *QIp*. What thoughts or feelings do you associate with this word? Any memories or fears? Jot down what comes up when you hear this word.

_____
_____
_____
_____

If you're like most people, far fewer associations came up with the second word. Unless you regularly practice the Klingon language from *Star Trek*, we're guessing not much came up at all. For those of you who, like us, are not fluent in Klingon, *QIp* translates to *stupid*. But since we don't associate memories or emotions with this word of the same meaning, it feels less real or true. Defusion is a bit like looking at your thoughts in a language you do not speak.

Think of defusion as the process of getting unstuck from thoughts by creating healthy distance from your internal experiences. You might ask, why not just change the thought altogether? Some types of therapies do attempt to change the content of thoughts by reframing them, assessing their accuracy, or practicing new thinking patterns. Unfortunately, much like what you learned in chapter 6 about the inefficacy of avoiding thoughts, changing the content of thoughts is often equally unproductive (Sauer & Baer, 2009). So rather than changing the content of a thought, cognitive defusion is the skill of changing your *relationship* to the thought.

Thoughts are merely a form of language occurring in your mind. While this means thoughts are vulnerable to the same traps as language, it also means you can use the power of language to get unstuck. Have you ever said or written a word so many times that it started to look or sound weirdly . . . wrong? Take the word *wrong*, for example. If we write WRONG in many different ways, Wrong might start to look a little *wrong*. Are we even spelling **Wrong** correctly anymore, or should *WRONG* look different? In fact, now that we think of it, is w r o n g even a real word?

If you're in a place where it's appropriate, try saying "wrong" out loud several times and see what happens. Does it sound like /rAHng/ or like /rOng/ or like /rawng/ or like we've broken the word W R O N G forever? This was an example of cognitive defusion. By making letters and sounds lose their meaning and salience, it is much more difficult to get stuck on them. If you were feeling stuck on having said the *wrong* thing recently for example, you're welcome! This simple exercise of defusing from the salience of "wrong" may have given you some healthy distance. In this next section, we cover specific strategies for practicing cognitive defusion.

Labeling Thoughts as What They Are: Thoughts

One simple exercise to create distance from your thoughts is to simply label them as "thoughts." This may sound overly simplistic, but trust us: This is a classic ACT technique for practicing cognitive defusion. For example, if you have a thought that gives you a strong reaction, such as *If I speak up in this meeting, they'll know I'm not as competent as I appear*, try purposely thinking it again as *I'm having the thought that if I speak up in this meeting, they'll know I'm not as competent as I appear*. Or you could say, *My mind is telling me that I'm not competent, and speaking up in this meeting will show that*.

Another example might be noticing a thought like *My coworker is so annoying, he would never understand* and saying instead, *I'm having the thought that my coworker is annoying, and my mind is telling me that he won't understand what I'm going through*. While this is a simple strategy, it does require you to notice when thoughts or feelings show up that you might be fused with. This is why we chose to present our chapter on mindfulness early on. If you're finding that you never get an opportunity to practice labeling your thoughts, it might be a sign that more practice around mindfulness is needed. Let's try an exercise to illustrate cognitive defusion.

Exercise—Picture Yourself

For this exercise, draw yourself in the space on the next page. This does not need to be a work of art. It can even be a stick figure. Just give it some distinguishing feature that makes it you. You can also tape a picture of yourself on the page if you prefer. Now, look at this picture of yourself and notice any thoughts, feelings, or sensations that you might be fused with. Write them down *over* the picture. Start with "I am . . ." for any thoughts about yourself. Write emotions and physical sensations where they seem to occur in the body.

Chapter 8: *Putting Things into Perspective*

For the second part of this exercise, draw or tape a similar photo of yourself in the new space on the following page. Around the space where your picture will be, there are thought bubbles. In them, write the same messages from your previous drawing, but use "I'm having the thought/feeling/sensation . . ." language at the start of each. Notice any reactions as you transfer the thoughts and experiences onto the page.

SAYING THE WRONG THING

What did you notice during the exercise? Did it feel different when you labeled your thoughts as thoughts instead of facts? How so? Perhaps you felt less tension, dread, or heaviness as a result? Chances are, you did because your relationship to the words changed, allowing you to adopt the stance of a casual observer of the thoughts rather than a cowering recipient beneath them. Taking your thoughts outside of your mind by saying them out loud or writing them down creates distance in and of itself.

Chapter 8: *Putting Things into Perspective*

Jess's Story—Having an Agenda

I am a queer, nonbinary social worker who has spent almost fifteen years working with transgender and gender-diverse youth and their families. I am often hyperaware of my position in my work with cisgender parents who are fearful or skeptical of my presence in the clinical relationship with their child and family. Many years ago, a parent accused me of having an agenda: trying to "force" her to support her child's gender identity. She felt that I was not being objective in my assessment of her child's experience, that I believed being trans was superior, and that I wanted to "contaminate" her child's identity. I used to think of the word *agenda* in neutral terms. But because of that interaction, that word now stings, resulting in thoughts of not being good enough and feelings of anxiety, sadness, and fear.

Since then, when I hear the word *agenda* in interactions with other youth and families, I sometimes remain silent to avoid a similar accusation, even though advocating for my client would be truer to my values. It is an ongoing challenge, but when I'm working with a parent who is skeptical or afraid, I now utilize cognitive defusion so that I am better equipped to take appropriate clinical actions that are aligned with my values. I like to imagine that I'm looking at the word *agenda* through foggy or frosted glass to get some helpful distance. Maybe I can't quite make it out. Maybe I see someone polishing the word to make it shine. Maybe I do have an agenda, but that is to help get young people to adulthood, and that is okay.

Thanking Your Mind

We all have an inner critic—that voice telling us all the reasons we are not good enough—and we can easily get stuck on the things it says. But have you ever wondered why it exists? Simply put, the inner critic exists because it believes its role is (however unhelpfully) to protect you and keep you safe. For example, the thought *I'm unlovable* may be serving a protective function that keeps you from entering into relationships that require vulnerability and the potential to get hurt. While this might prevent the pain that comes from heartbreak, it also precludes the joy and meaning that come from forming loving relationships.

When you can realize that your inner critic isn't *trying* to be mean—it's just trying to help you—this can provide some distance from your thoughts and foster self-compassion. For this reason, another classic defusion strategy in ACT involves noticing when you are having an unhelpful thought and thanking your mind for the attempt to help. Imagine a person who thinks *I don't want to be a burden* every time they need help with a task. By noticing this thought, the person can say to themselves, *Thank you, mind—I can see you're trying to prevent me from ever feeling like I am a burden, but that thought is not helpful right now because it's important that I seek help in this situation.* Shortened, this strategy can look like a genuine "Thank you, but not right now" when distracting, inaccurate, or harmful thoughts arise.

The Improv Method

If you have ever heard anything about improv acting, you've probably heard the importance of the phrase *yes, and*. The purpose of the phrase in the context of improv is to keep a scene moving. If your acting partner says something absurd and you say "no" or shut it down, the scene doesn't have anywhere to go and something brand new must happen. However, by saying "yes, and" you are accepting the premise of what your acting partner says and adding to it, thus moving the scene along.

So, what does this have to do with cognitive defusion? The key is to look for thoughts that contain the word *but* and to replace them with *and*. Not only will this actually be more accurate most of the time, it will also facilitate getting unstuck. For example, a parent might have the thought *I want to spend more time with my kids, but I'm so busy with work.* Here, the word *but* suggests that these two statements are mutually exclusive, though they are not. Does the parent want to spend more time with their kids? Yes! (And!) The parent is also so busy with work. While this doesn't change the facts, it diminishes the power of the thought "too busy," which invalidates the parent's feelings about wanting to have more time as a family. It also may foster creative problem-solving around spending more time with family *despite* being busy.

The Benefits of Getting Unstuck

As with the other processes described in this workbook, you don't have to take it from us that getting a healthy distance from thoughts is helpful. Remember our adventure with the word *wrong*? (Wroooooooong . . . yes, it definitely sounds normal now, right?) In one study, experimenters compared the act of rapidly repeating a word (like *wrong*) to other thought control and distraction strategies; they found that simply repeating a word or phrase over and over again was effective in making self-critical thoughts feel less unpleasant and less believable (Masuda et al., 2004).

Chapter 8: *Putting Things into Perspective*

Another study found similar changes when participants were instructed to say, "I'm having the thought that . . ." in addition to singing the thought to the tune of "Happy Birthday" and saying the thought in funny voices (Larsson et al., 2016). And lest you think your thoughts are far too self-critical for these simple techniques, even adults high in self-criticism were found to benefit from a mobile app that taught them defusion strategies (Levin et al., 2018).

> ## Danielle's Story—Not Compassionate Enough
>
> I started my career as a pediatric psychologist shortly before the onset of the COVID-19 pandemic. After more than a decade of training, I was finally ready to do the job I cared about. Then came 2020. Between working from my bedroom in Portland, Oregon, intense social unrest, wildfires, and more, I started to feel burned out and struggled to find empathy (an important trait for a psychologist!). I felt angry toward other people who seemed to choose their own comfort over the health of all people. I felt angry toward myself for "not being compassionate enough." I was irritable with people I cared about and even more irritable with myself.
>
> At a time when I could have benefited from social support, I was explicitly avoiding having conversations with friends or family. I was convinced my sudden irritability and lack of empathy would lead me to saying something I would regret. This is an example of a time I was very fused with some of my thoughts, particularly around not being compassionate enough. At one point, I started to notice a pit in my stomach every time my phone lit up with a text message or call. I was no longer engaging in things I enjoyed, not because I wasn't interested, but because I was so drained every day from work. Constantly trying to prove to yourself that you are compassionate enough is hard work, after all. Something was clearly wrong.
>
> Though it was unpleasant, I started to pay a little more attention to exactly what thoughts and feelings were coming up throughout the day. Eventually, I recognized how stuck I had become, and the paradoxical isolation I was creating for myself as a result. I started to thank my mind for its gallant efforts to protect me and my loved ones. I acknowledged that the context in which I was "losing empathy" was one of heightened stress for most people worldwide. I started labeling these unhelpful thoughts as thoughts, especially when they threatened to get in the way of connecting with others. While my struggles did not completely go away, these actions allowed me to reconnect with friends and family and to prioritize the aspects of my job that were most consistent with what brought me there in the first place.

SAYING THE *WRONG* THING

Flexible Perspective-Taking

Imagine for a moment that I am holding a red ball, and that you (wonderful reader) are holding a green ball. Now for the tricky part. If I were you and you were me, what color ball would you be holding? If you said a red ball, great job! Let's try another one. I am sitting *here* in a red chair, and you (dear reader) are sitting *there* in a green chair. If I were you and you were me, and here were there and there were here, what color chair would you be sitting in? Did you say a green chair? That's right, you're still in the green chair!

This may seem to be a simple exercise, but it is only possible because of the language capabilities you have been developing and strengthening from a very young age. Your ability to see things from different perspectives becomes more complex over time such that you can imagine what another person might be thinking and feeling even when they have not told you. As you have come to see with most of these skills, this one has both advantages and disadvantages.

Similar to cognitive fusion, *inflexible* perspective-taking can get you stuck on specific perceptions of yourself or others. For example, perhaps you are a parent, sibling, friend, teacher, spouse, baseball player on a local adult league, member of a marginalized group, *and* an extreme couponing enthusiast. (If you happen to be this exact combination of identities, please write to us and let us know!) Normally, you might realize that you certainly are not just one of these—and you aren't even just the combination of these—but when you are stressed or under pressure, you might get stuck on one idea about yourself, or on the implications of one idea. A common example is when people get stuck on what they perceive as the worst thing about themselves. Failed marriage. Medical burden. Bad friend. Loser. Alcoholic. Unfaithful. Broken.

Similarly, you can get stuck on narrow conceptualizations of others. Maybe you've had thoughts, or even heard others say something, like any of the following: "Our boss is too clueless to ever understand why diversity efforts matter." "Your partner is just a control freak." "This coworker gaslights everyone." "My neighbors are crazy." "These elected officials are just corrupt." "People of that generation are such a problem." "People of this political affiliation are all [woke / inhumane / insert derogatory term here]." As you can see, it's possible to get stuck on one idea for whole groups of people!

As with cognitive fusion, you can get stuck on positive conceptualizations of yourself and others as well. Is identifying as an extreme couponing enthusiast necessarily a bad thing? Of course not. But if failing to save a certain amount of money causes you severe

Chapter 8: *Putting Things into Perspective*

distress, or if maintaining the couponing lifestyle is getting in the way of important relationships, then your relationship to that identity may be a problem. And if you get stuck on the idea that this particular aspect of your identity is important, it will be harder to give this activity up even if it starts to interfere with your personal values.

> ### Jess's Story—Perspectives Frozen in Time
>
> I could write an entire book on binary thinking, especially when it comes to gender, but for this story, I want to talk a little bit about my work with transgender and gender-diverse (TGD) youth and their families. From the time we are born (or even before then, if expecting parents choose to view the ultrasound results), assumptions are made about our sex and, consequently, what our gender identities, roles, and expressions might be. From the moment parents hear "It's a ____!" they form a narrative in their minds, whether conscious or not, about who this child will be and what they might look like. And then there's the process of naming a child! Often, this is a painstaking process that has been approached with great care, and the decided-upon name has great meaning. It is rare that a parent will look at a newborn and think, *What if my expectations are wrong or unfair for this child?* (Obviously expectations go beyond gender identity, but stick with me!)
>
> Therefore, when a TGD person comes out to the adults in their life and discloses their true gender identity, the clash of perspectives and expectations often causes tensions to arise. TGD people often have had months or years to get to the point of accepting themselves and may find it difficult to take the perspective of adults who react with fear, questioning, lack of affirmation, and so on. They may not recognize that the adults need some time to catch up. On the flip side, adults may find it difficult to take the perspective of the TGD person, especially since the most important adults in a TGD person's life are often cisgender and don't feel like they have a frame of reference to adequately take perspective. Not to mention the impact of society on ideas about gender for everyone involved. It can almost feel like perspectives are frozen in time.
>
> This dynamic can lead families to get stuck in their ability to align and to see the many areas in which they do agree and have mutual understanding. In these situations, my role as an outside party is to be the mirror for each perspective, with the goal of helping TGD youth and adults shift in their perspectives and move forward together.

SAYING THE *WRONG* THING

Exercise—I Am

Below you will see numbers 1 through 10, each with the sentence stem "I am . . ." For this exercise, think about yourself and how you see yourself in relation to others. Once you have reflected on this, complete each statement below with the first words or phrases that come to mind. It is best to do this exercise quickly rather than dwelling on any one answer.

1. I am _____.
2. I am _____.
3. I am _____.
4. I am _____.
5. I am _____.
6. I am _____.
7. I am _____.
8. I am _____.
9. I am _____.
10. I am _____.

Once you have completed all ten items, take a moment to reflect on your answers. You might notice if your answers were more often adjectives (e.g., "I am kind"), nouns (e.g., "I am a sister"), or temporary states of being (e.g., "I am sad"). Were your answers more stable traits, or things that shift and change over time? Were your statements mostly positive, negative, or mixed? How did your answers relate to how you interact with others? Reflect on whether it was easy to generate answers or if it took some effort.

_____
_____
_____
_____
_____

Now that you have reflected on the experience, you are going to do a few things to your list. First, cross out the statement you listed for #2. Yes, we are serious! Go ahead and

Chapter 8: *Putting Things into Perspective*

put a line right through it. Now, for #7, put a caret (this symbol: ^) between "I am" and the rest of your statement and insert the word *not*. Stay with us here. For #4, change the punctuation at the end of the statement to an exclamation mark (!). And finally, for #10, underline a word in the sentence of your choosing.

How did that feel? If it felt weird, why do you think so? What thoughts or feelings showed up for you? If you had any strong reactions to changing the items, reflect on whether there are aspects of yourself (or your relationships with others) that you might be fused to. Write your reactions below.

_____
_____
_____
_____
_____

In reality, this exercise involved making squiggles on paper that have no real bearing on your actual life. And yet, we are so attached to the labels we give ourselves that the simple act of drawing a line through some squiggles can feel gut-wrenching. (The first time Danielle did this exercise, #2 said "I am a sister" and she refused to put a line through it! Thankfully, she has become more flexible since then.) But squiggles on a page can bear enormous weight due to the power of language. Fortunately, language is also a powerful tool that we can use in our favor. By making simple changes to our language, we can gain distance and perspective. Flexible perspective-taking involves creating distance from our rigid self-attributes that get in the way of following our values, both positive and negative. It involves seeing ourselves and others as greater than the sum of our parts, as whole human beings with a diverse array of life experiences, skills, joys, and mistakes.

To practice this skill, we offer several strategies in this chapter that help you see yourself from a broader perspective, recognizing that you are not defined by any one concept or idea. Other strategies will help you perspective-take to view others as similarly whole humans who transcend their characteristics and experiences. Let's briefly review these strategies here.

SAYING THE *WRONG* THING

The Self-as-Context

Think for a moment about an experience you had today, any experience at all. Hold it in your mind and reflect on what your surroundings looked like at the time, how you were feeling, and any thoughts you were having.

_____
_____
_____

Now, think about something that happened to you last year, and reflect on some of the same aspects of your experience.

_____
_____
_____

Finally, think of a memorable experience you had as a child, before the age of ten. Again, reflect on your surroundings, who else was there, what you could see or hear at the time, and any strong feelings or thoughts you can remember having.

_____
_____
_____

Now, think about yourself in each of these three memories. You were different ages, probably looked a little different, and likely had different feelings and thoughts. But what about you was the same? First and foremost, you were *you* each time. You were experiencing things through your same senses and observing your surroundings from the vantage point of you. In fact, you have been *you* your whole life! You are the observer of your experiences, whether good or bad or unmemorable—you were there *then* just as you are here *now*.

In ACT, this aspect of humanity is called the "observing self," and it is meant as a reminder that you can always step back to notice your experiences because you are the *context* in which your experiences happen. And the "you" who is the forever-observer of

Chapter 8: *Putting Things into Perspective*

your experiences is greater than the sum of its parts. Rather than being defined by any single characteristic, positionality, or experience, you are the context in which those exist.

The Self-as-Process

In the same way that you can notice yourself as a context for your experiences, you can also experience the self as an ongoing *process*. You can take a step back and notice your experiences *in the moment* as they are occurring. Often, you might be pulled to evaluate those experiences as "good" or "bad" or something else. By building a flexible "self-as-*process*," you notice thoughts, feelings, and other parts of yourself as they are in the moment, without changing or evaluating them. This may sound a lot like mindfulness, and it is! The concepts you're learning here are interconnected and build upon one another.

Others-as-Context and Others-as-Process

If you are a context for your experiences—and you also experience the self as an ongoing process of observing the world—it goes without saying that other people are and do, as well. Everyone has a sense of self that is greater than the sum of their parts, experiences, or characteristics, forever in process as time goes on. Sometimes, it is easy to see others as a limited set of characteristics and behaviors, which can contribute to conflict. For example, if an employee primarily sees their boss as demanding and unhelpful, they are more likely to perceive interactions with their boss through that lens. There might be a scenario where the boss offers the employee a task to help make the case for promotion. But seen through the lens of a boss who is "demanding and unhelpful," the employee might perceive the task as just another thing that has unnecessarily fallen into their lap.

Similarly, if a person sees their neighbor putting up a campaign sign in their yard or wearing clothing representing an opposing political affiliation, the person may assume the neighbor is intolerant or narrow-minded. If the same neighbor presents as kind and engaging—offering to share a meal, perhaps—the person may not notice or appreciate the authenticity of this gesture due to their expectation that the neighbor holds inherently opposing views. By seeing others as full and whole humans with complex histories and experiences, we invite curiosity and openness into the conversation.

SAYING THE *WRONG* THING

Exercise—Whole Human Being

Take a moment to think about something you've been stuck on lately—about either yourself or someone else. Complete the following sentences based on this stuckness to practice taking a more flexible perspective.

Lately, I've been very stuck on the belief that _____
("I am" or "This person is")

_____. While it can be hard to let go sometimes, the truth is, we are
(attribute you've been stuck on)

all human and greater than the sum of our parts. _____
("I am" or "This person is")

a whole human being, with many other qualities, hopes, fears, and experiences. For

example, _____ is just one of many things
(attribute you've been stuck on)

about _____ that people should know.
("me" or "this person")

_____ also _____. I will
("I am" or "This person is")   (other attributes or identities)

try to keep this in mind next time I feel stuck on _____.
(attribute you've been stuck on)

Once you're done, read the sentences back to yourself and reflect on any feelings or other experiences that come up.

_____

_____

_____

_____

_____

_____

Chapter 8: *Putting Things into Perspective*

Steph's Story—The Imperfect Conversation

I didn't realize how many emotions would come up when I wrote the vignette in chapter 6 regarding the pediatric oncology patient. I was teeming with unreasonable frustration and resentment that our patient never had the opportunity for an honest and dignified conversation about end-of-life planning. I also had conflicting thoughts about my own role and what I could have done differently: "I should have advocated more." "But I couldn't advocate more because then I'd be out of my lane." "I guess I could have brought it up more diplomatically?" "But actually, no way, there was already tension about roles, and it's the team's role to do that." "But what is my role?" "If people appreciated my expertise more, it would have been easier for me!" "The conversation didn't happen, and that's on all of us, not just me!" "There's nothing I could have done differently to make them understand—I just failed."

I shared these frustrations with a close friend, debating whether the team or I was responsible for the patient not having a conversation about end-of-life care. Ultimately, I believed that my anger had gotten in the way of my ability to clearly communicate with the team. My friend gently interrupted my thought process. "It sounds like what you are saying is that since the conversation didn't happen exactly the 'right' way, then you failed."

This left me speechless. It was true. I believed that because the conversation hadn't happened exactly how and when I'd recommended, I had failed. The team had failed. We were all failures. In reality, the conversation likely did happen after the patient's hospice admission, and the family was likely more prepared for it because of my and the team's efforts. I also realized that my anger was not the only barrier to better communication and action. Fear played a bigger role. My fear that these painful conversations "must be exactly right, or we failed" was a driving force to my avoidance *and* theirs.

Having this conversation with my friend allowed me to shift my perspective on two important facts. First, I am not a failure just because something didn't happen exactly how I thought it should. Maybe I actually did an okay job. Maybe even a good job. Second, the team is not a failure just because they didn't make something happen exactly how I thought they should. Maybe they are actually doing an okay job. Maybe even a really good job.

Next time, my advice to the team (and to myself!) will be to have compassion and understand that there is no "perfect" way or time to have these conversations. Having the conversation at all is immeasurably more important than having a "perfect" conversation. I can empathize with the fear of imperfection and remind myself and others that our fears are scarier than reality . . . even when reality *is* scary and horribly sad.

SAYING THE *WRONG* THING

Jess's Exercise—Taking a Walk in Their Shoes

In this exercise, you'll be asked to reflect on a challenging interpersonal situation leading to disconnection or misunderstanding and then practice flexible perspective-taking. This is intended to help you to see the other person as a full and complex human being, to consider how you may have been perceived and what you wish had been understood instead, and to identify what skills you might have applied to promote understanding and connection. You will also elicit feedback from an outside party to broaden your perspective even further.

To begin, think about a recent conversation or situation in which there was conflict or both parties felt misunderstood. Briefly describe the scenario here.

_____
_____
_____
_____
_____

Now take some time to reflect on what important perspectives you and the other person may have missed in the conversation. On the first pair of shoes, write down what you wish the other person would have understood about your perspective. On the second pair of shoes, write down what the other person may wish you had understood.

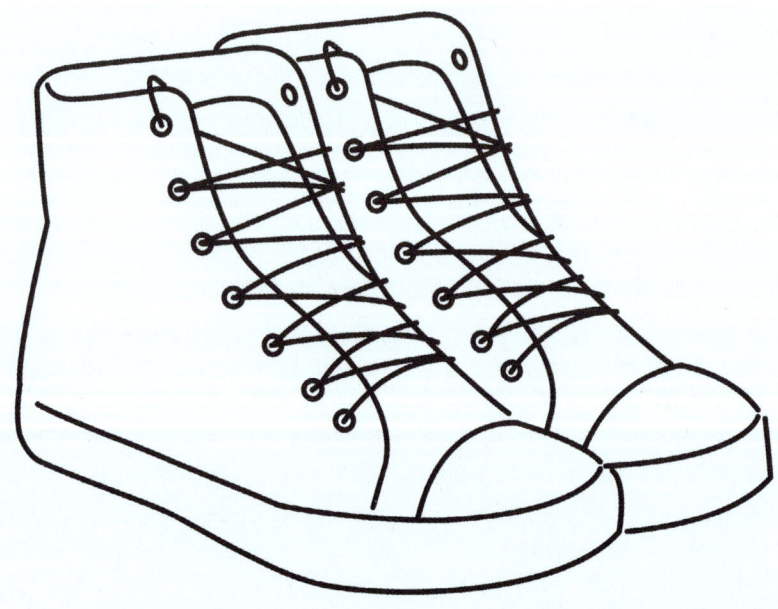

Chapter 8: *Putting Things into Perspective*

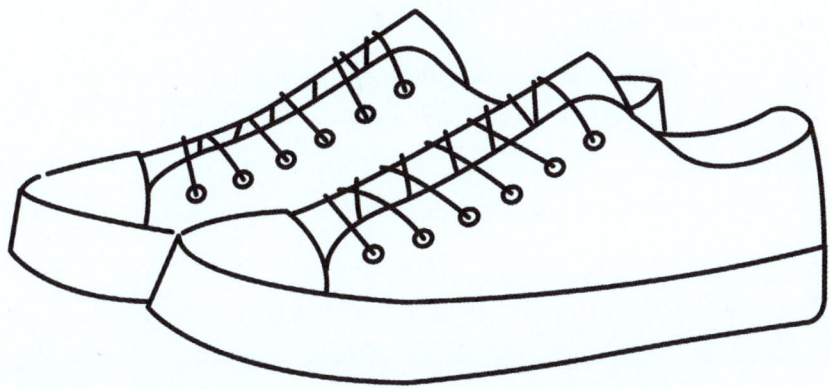

Thinking about what you've learned so far in this book, what skills do you think could have helped you or the other person understand each other's perspectives better? For example, would it have helped to be more connected to the present moment? Would being clear about your values and being curious about the other person's values have promoted a different interaction? Were you having trouble with willingness and needing more strategies for managing distressing thoughts and feelings? Were you getting fused with certain thoughts and needing to get distance from them? Were you struggling with perspective-taking and needing help seeing the other person as a whole human who is more than the conflict you were having?

_____
_____
_____
_____
_____

For an extra challenge, discuss this conflict with a friend or other trusted person. Tell them about the situation and share any insights you gleaned from taking a walk in the other person's shoes. Invite your friend to provide honest feedback on the situation, as well as your conclusions about your own perspective and that of the other person. Reflect on anything you learned from the conversation with your friend here.

_____
_____
_____

SAYING THE *WRONG* THING

The Benefits of Flexible Perspective-Taking

The benefits of perspective-taking are innumerable if you're looking for a more effective way to resolve internal (and external!) conflicts. But don't just take our word for it—the research bears this out as well. For example, studies have found that having a more flexible sense of self is associated with positive mental health outcomes (Moran et al., 2018), as well as improved social functioning (Şahin et al., 2022), while more inflexible perspective-taking is associated with a variety of negative mental health outcomes, including depression and anxiety (Pakenham et al., 2023). Research has also shown that interventions aimed at improving flexible perspective-taking are effective. For example, even taking a simple five-minute training on the "self-as-context" has been found to buffer against the impacts of stress (Godbee & Kangas, 2022).

> ### Danielle's Story—Taking Your Mind on a Date
>
> I work primarily with transgender youth. One of my patients was a young adult transgender male who had been taking testosterone for several years and had recently finished recovering from top surgery. For so long, he felt that his life was consumed by trying to obtain the medical interventions he needed to feel affirmed in his gender, completing document after document to legally change his name and gender marker, and all while trying to pass high school, get into college, save money, and maintain friendships.
>
> Now that he had completed his gender transition goals and felt comfortable with his college classes and work schedule, he thought about dating for what felt like the first time. He downloaded a few dating apps and started to put together a profile but didn't get much further than his name and gender. Every time he picked up his phone to work on his profile, his mind started to chatter. Should his profile indicate that he was transgender, or should he wait until he knew someone better before disclosing this information? Would it even be safe to indicate this information on a profile or to go on a date without disclosing this? Should he be asking other people about their history with gender? Would he spend entire dates being distracted by all these questions? Would he say the wrong thing and ruin the date? And the question that always led to closing the app entirely: Would he ever be loveable?
>
> Over time and with acceptance and mindfulness strategies he learned in therapy, the patient acknowledged that his mind was trying to protect him with this chatter, but the costs of avoiding dating were becoming more and more clear. In particular,

Chapter 8: *Putting Things into Perspective*

the very act of avoiding dating was paradoxically reinforcing the "unlovable" narrative, and he was beginning to internalize stigma toward his own identity. With this knowledge, he decided to use defusion and perspective-taking techniques while setting up his dating profile. When the chatter started, he would thank his mind for trying to protect him. He would also label the different types of chatter as mythical creatures so he could acknowledge them individually. For example, there were elves (thoughts with questions that were worth considering the answers to), goblins (thoughts that were easy to get stuck on and not worth answering), sirens (thoughts that were pure avoidance or distraction), and of course the Demogorgon (any reference to being unlovable). He even drew them and labeled thoughts that were especially loud on paper so he could see them externally.

Another important part of our work in therapy was helping him recognize that he was more than just his transgender identity. Because so much of his energy had been directed toward his transition for so long, it was easy for him to get stuck on the idea that this identity defined him. We used mindfulness exercises so he could practice seeing himself as the context for his experiences and identities, noticing that his gender journey was only one of many things about his life and personhood. The patient started journaling about what qualities he was looking for in a partner, as well as how his own qualities were similar to or different from those he was looking for. Over time, he reflected on the benefits of seeing himself as an outside observer might, which allowed him to learn things about himself he may not have otherwise explored.

Although questions about when and how to disclose his transgender identity continued to come up, and issues of safety remained relevant, he was no longer paralyzed by these thoughts. He was able to start going on dates and begin developing this aspect of his life, even when his mind decided to tag along as a third wheel.

Exercise—Shifting Perspective

Think of a time when you were worried about saying the wrong thing or felt like you did say the wrong thing (or a current worry you have about saying the wrong thing in the future). If nothing comes to mind, you can use another thought that has interfered with or might interfere with an important conversation. Write about it in the space here or on a separate piece of paper. Try to be detailed about the thoughts and feelings that come up when you think about this experience, especially the fears or worries.

_____
_____
_____
_____
_____
_____

Now, think of a close friend or family member that you care about. Hold them in your mind for a few moments. For the second part of this exercise, read back what you wrote and try to hear it in your friend or family member's voice, as if they were telling you about an experience they had or will have. While reading it in their voice, reflect on whether any aspect of the story feels different. How do you feel toward your loved one after hearing their fears or worries? What advice might you offer them related to this situation?

_____
_____
_____
_____
_____
_____

Shifting Your Relationship with Saying the Wrong Thing

One of the reasons we combined these two processes (cognitive defusion and perspective-taking) into one chapter is that their overlap is particularly pronounced when it comes to helping with difficult conversations. Often, when discussing topics close to our hearts, we can feel as though our whole self is being challenged or undermined if the other person disagrees with or questions our beliefs. This leaves us at heightened risk of getting stuck. While there are many aspects of conversation we can get stuck on (e.g., our own thoughts, our sense of

Chapter 8: *Putting Things into Perspective*

self, or our perception of the other person), we named this workbook after the one we hear most often: saying the wrong thing. Fortunately, we can use the cognitive defusion and flexible perspective-taking skills learned in this chapter to approach these conversations with the "fear of saying the wrong thing" standing *by our side* instead of *in our way*.

Play and Practice

- Look back to chapter 1 and identify the topic or situation that brings up the most difficult thoughts or feelings for you. Identify the thought most likely to get in your way and write it down on a single sheet of paper in as many fonts, colors, and sizes as possible. Get creative with block letters, elaborate designs, and more. Reflect on your reaction to the painful thought or phrase after completing this activity.

- Keep a journal with you for a day; every time you or another person says "but" when you could really be saying "and," make a note in your journal. At the end of the day, reflect on the frequency of these unhelpful "buts" and whether there were themes connecting those topics.

- Think about a difficult conversation you may need to have in the future. Write a letter to the person you need to have the conversation with stating all the information you're hoping to get across. Describe any thoughts that come up for you with "I'm having the thought . . ." or "My mind is telling me . . ." language. When you're finished writing the letter, read it back to yourself, but imagine that it is coming from the other person, as if it were written to you instead. Reflect on how you receive the information that you are intending to give to someone else.

- With a trusted person, choose a topic that brings up mild distress. Set a timer for five minutes and discuss the topic, noticing any thoughts or feelings that come up along the way. After the five minutes are up, debrief with your partner by describing your experiences during the discussion (e.g., "I felt my heart start to race when I shared my stance on this topic. I noticed a lot of worry that you might regard me as a bad person. Even now, I'm having the thought that I wish I hadn't brought this up").

Takeaway Points

- Cognitive defusion is the skill of getting unstuck from thoughts, feelings, or body sensations by creating distance from their meaning.
- Simple defusion techniques include writing or saying a word repeatedly or in different ways, labeling thoughts as thoughts, thanking your mind, and replacing "but" with "and" when two parts of a thought are both true.
- Flexible perspective-taking is the skill of seeing yourself and others as whole human beings that hold a complex array of experiences, attributes, and identities, rather than getting stuck on a singular aspect.
- Flexible perspective-taking techniques include observing the self and others as a *context* for your experiences. By taking a step back, you can notice that you are greater than the sum of your parts.
- Flexible perspective-taking helps you develop open-mindedness to have meaningful, productive conversations.

CHAPTER 9

Finding Compassion for Yourself and Others

> "When love meets suffering and stays loving, that's compassion."
>
> —Zen Buddhist saying

You have come so far in your journey of showing up to difficult conversations. Throughout this book, we have prompted you to be kind to yourself amid difficult thoughts and emotions. Let's finally delve into the details of taking a compassionate stance. As you know, this work is *hard*. It is easy to be judgmental, defensive, closed off, and ashamed. If you have been taught to put others first or to hold yourself to high standards of emotional control, even the mention of compassion or self-compassion can be an immediate turn-off, so we've waited until now to focus on this skill. Many people incorrectly associate these terms with weakness or making excuses, but by now you hopefully realize that taking a compassionate stance for yourself and others actually requires incredible courage and strength!

In this chapter, you will learn what it means to show compassion for yourself and others. As always, we will provide you with opportunities to practice in this workbook and in your daily life. Depending on your upbringing and personal history, you may find one or the other more challenging, so pay attention to what shows up for you and where you may need more practice.

Defining Compassion and Self-Compassion

Broadly speaking, compassion involves both recognizing and desiring to relieve or prevent another person's emotional pain or suffering (Gilbert, 2017). Self-compassion, on the other hand, is the process of turning that compassion inward. It involves treating yourself with the same care and kindness that you would extend a good friend, especially in the face of failures or setbacks (Neff, 2003). Although it is not possible to prevent or "fix" all emotional pain, actively turning toward it does fundamentally change the experience. As with mindfulness, compassionate action requires you to step away from judgment into a broader sense of awareness.

Compassion is a concept as old as human thought and is fundamentally rooted in our evolution as social creatures. Our brains are even programmed to build and facilitate compassion. Imaging studies have found that practicing compassion activates similar areas of the brain as when people experience meaningful social connection or love, which are physically and emotionally adaptive experiences that the brain tries to promote as much as possible (Klimecki & Singer, 2017). In addition, many contemplative, philosophical, and religious traditions have long revered compassionate practice as central to their teachings. For example, Buddhist and Jain traditions encourage compassion with an emphasis on alleviating and not causing suffering in others. Muslim and Christian traditions similarly teach individuals to build caring and supportive communities through compassionate treatment of others.

Compassionate practices are often taken out of their historical and cultural contexts within the field of psychology, so it is important to recognize that while modern psychologists are conducting new research and finding new ways to make compassionate practices accessible to everyone, these concepts are age-old. You can probably think of lessons you have been taught about compassion throughout your own life. What definitions are you familiar with? What comes to mind when you think of compassion?

_____

_____

_____

_____

Chapter 9: *Finding Compassion for Yourself and Others*

Acting Versus Feeling

Compassion goes beyond feeling and is rooted in action, though both can occur at the same time. You've probably had this experience when caring for a sick or injured child or animal. You likely *felt* moved to ease their suffering while simultaneously being able to administer the physical care they needed. *Feeling* and *doing* do not always have to align, however. You can *feel* anger toward someone and simultaneously *act* with compassion toward them. When we say "act," we are not just referring to external actions (i.e., what you say or do). We are also referring to internal actions (i.e., what you say to yourself *about* a situation or person—these are the actions you take in your mind to consider multiple variables and perspectives). In this way, thoughts and feelings are also behaviors; seeing them as such can promote clarity.

Acting with compassion involves several components. First, it involves using mindfulness to differentiate your thoughts from your feelings, and noticing when these have automatically arisen based on past experiences. Second, it involves courageously turning toward the shared human experience of suffering and recognizing it as a natural part of life. (Here, it is helpful to use your new skills of letting go of control and having the willingness to show up!) Finally, acting with compassion involves choosing to care for yourself and others in your actions, even if you are not having caring *feelings* (more on this soon).

To explore each component, let's identify a simple example that is not too emotionally charged to build upon as we go. We will tackle challenging conversations again in later sections. Take a breath, relax your shoulders, and think of a recent situation that was uncomfortable for you, maybe even a little cringey. Perhaps you made a mistake at work and beat yourself up about it. Maybe you feel ashamed of raising your voice at your kid when they really pushed your buttons. Find an example that has some weight but won't overwhelm you. Describe the general situation in one sentence here.

_____
_____
_____
_____

Now that you've identified a scenario, let's walk through how it applies to each of the three components of *acting* with self-compassion.

SAYING THE *WRONG* THING

First Component: Differentiating Internal Experiences

Acting with self-compassion begins with an awareness that you are experiencing something painful. You can then work to understand and organize your internal experiences in a more workable way. To begin this process, notice and name at least three emotions that show up for you now as you think back on the cringey moment you just wrote about. These might include anger, fear, anxiety, pain, sadness, grief, or disgust.

_____

_____

_____

What are the thoughts associated with this example? Likely, these reflect some kind of automatic evaluation, such as *I suck! / I'm a terrible parent. / I'll never get this right.*

_____

_____

_____

_____

These automatic thoughts are rooted in previous experiences, including cultural background, economic and environmental circumstances, childhood events, the messages you have internalized from the media, and social interactions (both positive and negative). Can you follow the thread from these automatic thoughts back to your previous experiences? This may seem like a lot to do, but the more you practice, the more easily you will see familiar patterns emerge. Slowing things down in this way stops you from automatically falling into patterns of fight, flight, freeze, or fawn (chapter 6) and gives you the space and energy to make values-based choices. Make note of where these automatic thoughts might originate from in your learning history.

_____

_____

_____

_____

Chapter 9: *Finding Compassion for Yourself and Others*

Second Component: Turning Toward Suffering

Now that you've identified the emotions, thoughts, and threads of old learning, all that pain should feel a little more approachable. It's normal to want to escape it—*and* at the same time, suffering is a normal part of life. We all manage ups and downs in various ways, but instead of giving suffering all the power, let's do something about it. Remember that turning toward suffering is an act of courage. Although many cultures reward us for avoiding conflict, glossing over pain, or sweeping discomfort under the rug, by now you have learned that avoidance isn't always the answer.

While it sounds scary, sometimes turning toward your own suffering is as simple as what you just did: naming painful thoughts and feelings and acknowledging your learning history. It also helps to recognize that your suffering is tied to many things over which you had no choice or control. You did not choose where you were born, who your caregivers were, how your genetics are expressed, what school you went to, and so on. The suffering you are feeling now as you think back on your example is a result of many such factors. Take a big breath in . . . and let it out with an audible sigh.

What were some of the factors outside of your control that may have led you to this unsettling moment? Some may be historical. Perhaps you experienced childhood trauma that altered your nervous system, making it difficult to perspective-take or regulate yourself in upsetting situations. Maybe you grew up in an under-resourced family or area and weren't exposed to as much peace, play, or opportunity as other children. Perhaps you experience neurodivergent traits that render certain tasks more difficult than they are for your neurotypical peers. Other factors may have been unique to the moment: physical illness, stress caused by another event transpiring simultaneously in your life, and so on. Take a moment to consider these factors.

_____
_____
_____
_____
_____

Additionally, there may have been some factors within your control that contributed to this experience. Perhaps you skipped a meal, went to bed too late, consumed substances, or allocated time poorly. Can you take accountability (without blame or shame) for the elements that you may have been responsible for?

_____
_____
_____
_____

Remember that suffering is a normal and inevitable part of the human experience. It is easier to feel kindness, warmth, and care toward others and yourself when you recall that we are not alone in the roller coaster of life. Being sensitive to suffering does not excuse hurtful behaviors and choices, but it does promote objectivity and allow you to see situations with nuance. With that in mind, can you think of anyone in the entire world who may have had a similar reaction or made a similar mistake to yours at some point?

_____
_____
_____
_____

Third Component: Choosing to Engage in Caring Behaviors

We all have innate, biologically programmed drives that guide our behaviors and choices. For example, we are all programmed to avoid harm and seek food. We are programmed to care for those within our close social circles. We are programmed to handle injured children with gentleness—speaking to them in a soothing tone and tending to their physical needs— to promote the survival of the species. While this instinct to care can be interrupted by trauma and systemic oppression, it is something we are all born with. We are asking you to access this instinct to practice compassion. No, we are not asking you to hug the person arguing with you about social justice. We are asking you to see the other person (and yourself) as a human being whose own suffering has impacted their present moment.

Think back to your cringey example once more. As you recall this incident, notice how your body reacts to the memory. What happens to your muscles? Do you tense up,

Chapter 9: *Finding Compassion for Yourself and Others*

clench your jaw, or ball your fists? What about your posture? Do you have the urge to curl up or retract your body? What happens to your breath? Take some time to reflect on the reactions you would see if you looked in a mirror.

_____
_____
_____
_____

Notice the tone you take with yourself as you internally narrate the event. Is your tone warm, forgiving, and understanding, or is it critical, accusatory, and insensitive? Are you treating yourself with care or with contempt?

_____
_____
_____

Now, imagine that someone you care deeply about had engaged in this same cringey behavior. Imagine that you witnessed this happen and they turned to you for support. Who is this person? Write their name or relationship to you.

_____
_____

What body language would you demonstrate toward this person?

_____
_____
_____

What tone would you take toward this person?

_____
_____
_____

SAYING THE *WRONG* THING

What words or gestures would you use to demonstrate care?

_____
_____
_____

What do you notice about your response to this person compared to how you have responded to yourself?

_____
_____
_____

Hopefully, it felt relatively natural for you to cultivate care and compassion toward someone close to you. This is the same kindness you can extend to yourself in moments of difficulty. Read back through your cringey example once more, but this time approach yourself with the same tone and physical stance you just imagined for someone else. What is it like to relive this experience through the lens of self-compassion?

_____
_____
_____

If compassion does not come naturally to you, rest assured that like any other skill, it can be taught, learned, and honed. This next exercise will help you cultivate self-compassion by turning the compassion we more easily feel for others inward.

Exercise—Letters to a Friend

Recall a recent conversation that was difficult. Maybe the conversation went well, but you wish you had said additional things; maybe it did not go as you had hoped. Either way, write about the conversation as if you were describing it in a letter to someone, but to no one particular person. Write about the facts of what happened as well as any thoughts or feelings that you had at the time, that you've had since the conversation, and even that may be coming up now as you write the letter. Feel free to write as much as you'd like and use as much paper as you need. You can write this letter on a separate piece of paper so that it feels more authentic, or you can use the space on the next page.

Chapter 9: *Finding Compassion for Yourself and Others*

Once you are finished with the letter, write "Dear [*your name*]" at the very top. Yes, *your* name. Now, set the letter aside and think of someone you care about, such as a close friend, a sibling, a partner, or someone else. Once you have a person in mind, sign your letter with "Sincerely, [*their name*]" at the bottom. You can even fold the letter up as if it just arrived in the mail for the full effect. If you find this step difficult, you are not alone! Use the mindfulness and acceptance skills you have learned to work through the discomfort.

Now, read your letter back to yourself, aloud if possible, imagining that it came from the important person you identified. How do you feel about any judgments the letter describes? Do you find yourself wanting the person to know that their experiences are understandable and their judgments too harsh? Do you notice a desire to comfort this person? See if you can show yourself the same compassion you would show someone you care about. On the remaining free space of your paper (or below), write about any reflections you have after this exercise.

_____
_____
_____
_____
_____

What Compassion Is Not

Now that you've learned what compassion is and practiced cultivating that stance, it is important for us to clearly state what compassion is not. It is *not* weakness; it takes a great deal of courage and commitment to act with compassion. Compassion is also not a free pass or an excuse for hurtful behavior. You can hold yourself and others accountable with kindness and understanding for the pushes and pulls that influence behavior. Just because someone makes a bad *choice* does not mean they are a fundamentally bad *person*, even when they keep making that choice after receiving feedback again and again.

Self-compassion is also not a form of self-pity; it's the opposite! Self-compassion invites you to turn toward your pain with action, not complaints or whining. We often hear clients say that they are afraid they won't be able to hold themselves accountable or reach their goals if they exchange self-deprecation or painfully high expectations for compassion. On the contrary, compassion has been found to increase accountability and motivation

Chapter 9: *Finding Compassion for Yourself and Others*

(Breines & Chen, 2012). Self-compassion allows you to grow and learn from mistakes (rather than dwelling on or avoiding them), to decrease problematic perfectionism and increase both self-efficacy and confidence.

In addition, compassion is different from kindness, though they are related (Gilbert et al., 2019). While we can be simultaneously kind and compassionate, compassion is centered on actively attending to suffering, while kindness involves extending well wishes to ourselves or others. Empathy is also sometimes confused with compassion. While empathy is about *feeling* someone else's pain, compassion is about *acting* to alleviate their pain. Empathy is not necessarily a prerequisite for compassion, but it certainly can help!

The Importance of Compassion

Can you think of a time when you assumed someone intentionally meant you harm, only to later realize that it was a misunderstanding? When we feel backed into a corner or locked in battle with someone, our brains have this handy trick of jumping to conclusions. The human brain loves a good shortcut because it expends an enormous amount of energy to continuously interpret sensory input. So, if you are already feeling defensive or threatened, your brain will consolidate resources to make the quickest and safest assumption. Sometimes this is accurate, and sometimes it's way off base. Using a compassionate stance, in combination with the skills you've learned throughout this book, can lower your defenses and open your mind to exploring other possible interpretations and actions. It can also help you take responsibility for your role in challenging interactions without feeling overwhelmed by any negative feelings that might arise as a result (Leary et al., 2007).

There are many other benefits to compassion as well. For example, people who are more compassionate toward themselves and others tend to be more optimistic, more open to new experiences, and less anxious (Neff et al., 2007). Self-compassion can also help you counter your inner critic—that little voice that tells you exactly what you did or will do wrong in the future. With self-compassion, you can lower the volume on the inner critic and show up as your full, true self, especially when it counts. To do this, you first need to be able to recognize the critic, identify where it came from, and acknowledge the ways in which it has been trying to help you. That is the focus of this next exercise.

SAYING THE *WRONG* THING

Exercise—The Inner Critic

Make sure you are in a comfortable and private space for this exercise. Take a few centering breaths and settle your body into a comfortable and supported position. Now take some time to answer the following questions: In moments when you're disappointed in yourself, are there certain phrases that automatically come to mind? Phrases like "You'll never be good enough" or "You're pathetic"? What about any stories you play in your head again and again? Write these down here.

_____
_____
_____
_____

In what tone do you usually experience these words? Is the tone friendly? Critical? Belittling?

_____
_____

Does the voice of this critic seem familiar? Is it your own voice or the voice of someone else, such as a caregiver from early in life? Or do you perhaps experience this critic as certain images or sensations?

_____
_____
_____
_____

Do you remember where this inner critic learned to be so critical? Consider whether you internalized these messages from a family member, teacher, or other caregiver, or maybe even media or cultural influences.

_____
_____
_____
_____

Chapter 9: *Finding Compassion for Yourself and Others*

Give your inner critic a name. It can be something funny, serious, or literal. What fits for you?

_____
_____

What could this inner critic possibly be trying to protect you from? They all have a goal or purpose—what is yours?

_____
_____
_____
_____

Now, say something kind to your inner critic, using their name, and write it here. You can thank them for looking out for you or acknowledge the pain they carry. You know what they need to hear.

_____
_____
_____
_____

Take a few more deep breaths and stretch your body. It can be scary to approach your inner critic and address your suffering head-on. We encourage you to continue getting to know this inner critic in your daily life, taking time to notice how it influences your decisions and noting whether offering compassion opens new choices.

Nancy's Story—Compassionate Advocacy

If you have a disability or know someone with a disability, there are things you can't take for granted. You can't assume that people will understand the disability or act compassionately. If you're in a position of responsibility, like that of a caregiver, you will need to be an advocate or ally.

Parenting has been a journey of compassion for my neurodivergent daughter, myself, and the people I turned to for help. I had to find my voice so I could speak truth to power. From the moment my daughter was born, I saw that she was sensitive, intense, and reactive. She seemed bright but overwhelmed. When my daughter was one year old, we had our first conversation about suffering. I was in the kitchen washing dishes when she rushed over to me with a worried look on her face. She put her tiny hand on her heart and said "Owie . . . owie . . . owie."

I was confused. What was she trying to tell me? Then I heard a loud airplane passing over our house. I felt the subtle vibration in my body. I was stunned. How could the sound of an airplane cause such distress in my daughter? What did this mean? I didn't know what to say, so I hugged her and told her everything would be okay. I wanted everything to be okay, though I knew in my heart that things might not be okay. It was up to me to find out what was going on.

For many years, I had uncomfortable conversations with teachers, doctors, and specialists. Most of the time I felt dismissed, placated, and misunderstood. Eventually, my family arrived at an appropriate diagnosis and we were able to receive the support we needed.

As a parent, developing compassion eased the deep emotional pain of watching my daughter struggle to feel well and whole. Compassion motivated me to ease others' suffering by advocating for youth and families in my community. Over the course of my advocacy work, which has spanned thousands of difficult conversations, I have learned three things. First, I learned that you don't have to suffer in silence. Every conversation is an opportunity for growth and change. Compassionate conversations helped me accept the reality of being a marginalized parent with a marginalized child. I learned how to have self-respect amid ableism and other forms of bias. I learned how to speak up to insensitive teachers, doctors, and specialists who were gatekeepers to my daughter's care. I learned how to be compassionate with myself when I seethed with grief, fear, and rage over others' lack of compassion toward my daughter.

Second, I learned that you can find ways to have difficult conversations willingly and safely. Standing up for stigmatized needs and rights can feel emotional and vulnerable. For caregivers, not knowing what to say or do can feel scary and shameful. Despite those feelings, you can expand your communication skills and close

Chapter 9: *Finding Compassion for Yourself and Others*

> information gaps. When I'm going through a tough situation, I make time to reflect, consider my rights and responsibilities, plan out scripts and questions, and practice saying uncomfortable things so I feel less nervous and more prepared.
>
> Third, I learned that navigating difficult conversations is essential for compassionate leadership. Leadership comes in many forms, from leading by example to leading a group of people. I learned the hard way that—without compassion—we are vulnerable to caregiver burnout, advocacy fatigue, and conflict avoidance. Compassion can be liberating if it flows from a commitment to your values, not an inner voice of fear and frustration. During tough moments, try having a compassionate conversation with yourself. You can develop an internal "compassionate coach" who speaks to you in validating and motivating ways.
>
> What if we could normalize difficult conversations like sharing our struggles, speaking up, challenging the status quo, and advocating for what we need to thrive? What if courageous compassion were the norm? The world would be safer, kinder, and more inclusive for all of us.

Tapping into Your Emotions

Everyone experiences emotions differently. Some people experience emotions as parts of themselves (e.g., "Part of me is anxious and part of me is annoyed"), while other people experience emotions as different versions of themselves (e.g., "When I get angry, I act like a different person"). Sometimes, people can experience multiple layered emotions. For example, someone who is irritated on the surface can be tired, angry, scared, or sad underneath.

A huge part of developing compassion for yourself and others involves being able to experience the full range of emotions without getting too tangled in any one of them (there's that mindfulness stuff again!). During a heated argument, we often incorrectly assume that embodying feelings of hurt or anger will lend us an advantage, when—in reality—they can become traps. In these moments, it is more helpful to practice getting curious, which allows us to find distance from our emotions so we can choose how we want to act in the moment.

This is especially important when discussing topics close to our hearts. Rather than being pulled between logical debate points or feeling like a bleeding heart, compassion allows us to rest in an open posture where both logic and feeling are welcome and effective.

SAYING THE *WRONG* THING

Taking a curious stance and choosing to act with compassion helps slow those knee-jerk reactions, allowing us to act in ways that are consistent with our values. The following exercise will provide you with an opportunity to practice this.

Nancy's Exercise—Multiple Emotions

For this exercise, you'll be asked to connect with different emotions to discern how they sound and feel in your mind. Understanding how negative emotions affect your mind can help you decrease your inner struggle and increase mental clarity. Learning how to be motivated by self-compassion and compassion for others can help you break cycles of negativity and reactivity.

Don't worry if you can't tell the difference between your emotions (e.g., if you have trouble distinguishing anger from fear). You might be more familiar with some emotions than others. Just write down what you notice. You can also write down your physical sensations. Try to stay curious about what's going on inside you.

To begin, pick a recent conversation that made you feel upset or conflicted. Choose a conversation that brings up moderate discomfort, nothing too intense but not so minor that you can let go of it easily. What happened? How did the conversation affect you?

_____

_____

_____

Which aspects of the conversation bothered you the most?

_____

_____

_____

Now, see if you can connect to any feelings of anger or frustration about the conversation. For example, anger can sound critical or hostile. What does the voice of anger sound like to you? What does it say about you or the situation?

_____

_____

_____

Chapter 9: *Finding Compassion for Yourself and Others*

Next, see if you can connect to any feelings of fear or anxiety about the conversation. For example, fear and anxiety can sound worried or demanding. What does that voice sound like to you? What does it say about you or the situation?

_____
_____
_____

Then see if you can connect to any feelings of guilt or shame about the conversation. For example, guilt and shame can sound like blaming and doubting. What does that voice sound like? What does it say about you or the situation?

_____
_____
_____

Now, see if you can connect to any feelings of sadness, hurt, or grief about the conversation. The voice may be quieter and slower than the previous emotions. What does that voice sound like? What does it say about you or the situation?

_____
_____
_____

Finally, see if you can connect to a feeling of compassion. Compassion tends to sound like a warm and helpful voice. What does your compassionate self say about you or the situation? If you draw a blank, think about what a kind and wise person might say to you.

_____
_____
_____

Take a moment to look over your responses. What do you notice? How were your responses similar or different?

_____
_____
_____

SAYING THE *WRONG* THING

Which emotions were easier or harder to connect with?

___

How can you apply what you've learned to be more compassionate with yourself or others during difficult conversations or in general?

___

Exercise—Compassion for Another

The previous exercise helped you practice cultivating compassion within yourself. In the next exercise, you'll practice extending this sense of openness to someone you may not have positive feelings toward. Bring to mind a recent encounter that got you fired up. Maybe you tried to have a difficult conversation with someone, or maybe you heard about something this person said or did that was upsetting. Either way, pick a situation in which your emotions were high and you just *knew* the other person was wrong. Who is this person? Write their name or relationship to you.

___

What tone would (or did) you take toward this person?

___

What would (or did) your body language demonstrate toward this person?

___

Chapter 9: *Finding Compassion for Yourself and Others*

Now, take a moment to center yourself, focusing on your breath, your values, and all you've worked for to this point to answer this next set of challenging questions.

Can you imagine what this person might be afraid of that led them to behave this way?
___
___
___

What might their core values be?
___
___
___

Is there any chance you share some similar values but are choosing to move toward them differently?
___
___
___

What might this person have experienced in their past that could be influencing how they are behaving? Could there be any other factors influencing their behavior or choices?
___
___
___

With these in mind, can you connect to a sense of compassion here? What might your compassionate voice say about this person, in this situation?
___
___
___

SAYING THE *WRONG* THING

How was that? We know how difficult it can be to act with compassion toward someone you really disagree with, especially if you believe their position causes harm to others. At the same time, just because something is hard doesn't mean it's not important. In these times, remember to get curious about what you (and the other person) may be experiencing. You don't have to like the other person to see their humanity and connect with them compassionately.

Read that again: You don't have to like the other person to see their humanity and connect with them compassionately. Social change is impossible if you always have your fists up, ready for battle. While there is absolutely a time and place to fight, to make real and lasting change, we must learn to talk with one another.

Therefore, try to get curious instead. Doing so moves you into an engaged and open mindset from which you can act compassionately rather than defensively. You can supplement your curiosity with the foundational communication skills you learned in chapter 3. For example: "I think we're coming from really different backgrounds or stances here, and it's hard for me to see past that. Can you help me understand where you're coming from?" or "I almost feel like we are speaking different languages right now, but we have gotten along well in so many other conversations. What do you think could be getting in our way?"

Having a sense of curiosity can also help you determine how safe or workable a situation is. Sometimes, the compassionate choice is to walk away from a conversation, leaving it unresolved, or to set new boundaries in a relationship. Boundaries, as we see them, are not impermeable lines, but adjustable distances at which you can meet your own needs and respect the needs of others. So, if a conversation really is stuck, being curious and compassionate with this stuckness can tell you whether you need to change tactics (e.g., try some new communication skills, reconnect with the present moment or your values, have compassion for the other person's suffering) or perhaps kindly step away. Sometimes, the best way to show someone love and kindness is to choose *not* to have a painful conversation with them if they really aren't able to move forward with you. You can still address the pain you may feel for this person's stance, while recognizing that talking about it with them will never be productive. Compassion asks you to love people as they are, and this may mean redefining the quality or frequency of your interactions to maintain that love.

Chapter 9: *Finding Compassion for Yourself and Others*

Play and Practice

- Write a kind phrase that you can repeat to yourself daily. An example might be: "I'm a good person and am trying my best." If you like, you can write that phrase here to make it easy to remember: _____ _____. Do you notice anything shift in how you're talking to yourself throughout the day?

- Draw, paint, or sculpt what your inner critic looks like and place it somewhere you will see it every day. Practice literally turning toward this inner critic with words of kindness. If you get curious, why might your critic be treating you this way? What are they trying to protect you from? Can you thank them for their years of vigilant service and ask them to please step aside?

- Think about a recent situation that led you to feel bad about yourself. On a piece of paper, write out the details, sticking to the facts. Next, place pieces of translucent tape on top of these words, and with a different-colored pen or marker, write out judgments or self-criticisms that came to mind as you looked back (e.g., "You really messed up" or "I'm a bad friend"). Often, you'll find that these are words tied to shame or guilt. Take a step back and see how these layers can cloud your view of the situation, adding unnecessary suffering to an already difficult situation. Now peel away the tape and set it to the side, still in view. Choosing to see and set aside unnecessary suffering is an act of self-compassion.

- With a trusted person, examine recent news stories and take turns filling in the blanks about the people involved. What values might the parties have been acting on? What fears might they have been running from? Can you imagine other factors in their lives that led to their choices?

- With a trusted person, role-play treating each other with compassion. On different slips of paper, write brief conflict scenarios. Get specific. Examples might include disagreements about how to tip wait staff, how to handle a deceased family member's estate, or how to "correctly" load or unload the dishwasher. Draw a slip at random and practice engaging with each other in a compassionate manner. Give each other feedback on tone, body posture, and sense of openness.

- Practice being curious and compassionate in everyday scenarios. Keep a journal to track how many times throughout your day you automatically have a critical or negative reaction. In these moments, practice using a friendly voice to reframe the situation (or the person pushing your buttons) in a compassionate light.

SAYING THE *WRONG* THING

> ## **Takeaway Points**
>
> - Compassion is recognizing another person's suffering and desiring to actively ease that suffering. Self-compassion is turning that same compassion inward.
> - Acting with compassion involves several components: (1) learning to differentiate among your internal experiences, (2) turning toward suffering with courage, and (3) choosing to engage in caring behaviors even if you are not having caring feelings.
> - Compassion is *not* weakness, but an act of courage.
> - Compassion does not excuse bad behavior.
> - Approaching difficult conversations with compassion lowers your defenses and invites the other person to do the same, for the sake of meaningful connection.

CHAPTER 10

Saying the Wrong Thing with Purpose

> *"We have been too quiet for too long. There comes a time when you have to say something. You have to make a little noise. You have to move your feet. This is the time."*
>
> —John Lewis

Congratulations—you have finally reached the *committed* portion of acceptance and commitment therapy! You have been working hard to identify your "why" for stepping into meaningful conversations, to show up in the present moment with compassion for yourself and others, to understand the power of avoidance, and to disentangle from unhelpful rules and assumptions—gradually fitting each piece together and practicing within these pages and out in your life. Reaching this point means you've committed to a difficult and, at times, painful process. In this chapter, we will explore what it means to practice saying the wrong thing *with purpose*.

Defining Committed or Purposeful Action

In ACT, the term *committed action* is used to represent the actions you take that are informed by your values. However, this term can be misleading. Committed action is not an absolute, something you can succeed or fail at, or a one-time decision that lives on in perpetuity. Remember in chapter 2 when we introduced this concept and asked you to *try* to pick up a pen? Committed action is a moment-to-moment opportunity to make choices and take actions *in the direction of your values*. As the pen exercise demonstrated, we either act or don't act—there is no in-between (and yes, thinking can still be acting!). For this reason, we prefer the term *purposeful action*.

It can be challenging to think about small steps when we are well-trained to check things off lists and see the world in binary terms like success and failure. But guess what? The very act of picking up this book to engage in difficult conversations is a values-based choice that *you* made. Even if your practice so far hasn't always led to monumental changes, you have already been engaging in purposeful action! The other good news is that you cannot fail at purposeful action. No matter how many times you turn away in avoidance, every moment is a new opportunity to turn back toward your values. The compass you completed in chapter 5 can help remind you that your values are more of a direction and guide for your life than a checklist to complete. Purposeful actions are the concrete steps you take in the direction of your values.

Purposeful action, like values, is also sometimes confused with goals. Setting concrete goals is absolutely an important part of meaningful and sustainable behavior change. However, setting and achieving goals are only *components* of purposeful action, just like these actions are only components of moving toward values. Think back again to the pen exercise. You can have the goal of picking up a pen, but just setting that goal doesn't get the pen into your hand. Purposeful action occurs in the space between deciding and *doing*... again and again and again. It is not about loudly and skillfully speaking up against injustice every single time you see it occur. Purposeful action is about connecting with *why* speaking up is important to you and taking opportunities to do so, even if imperfectly or fearfully. And sometimes, it's about choosing not to speak up, if it doesn't feel right in the moment.

But we are not only talking about speaking out against injustice or concerns that lead to large-scale change. We are also talking about the small or seemingly inconsequential actions you take in every important or challenging conversation. The moments in which you show up with all your thoughts, feelings, and experiences to engage in dialogue that matters to you—those are moments of purposeful action.

Chapter 10: *Saying the Wrong Thing with Purpose*

Danielle's Story—**Not Cool, Bro**

There was a moment, years ago now, that I remember well today. I was scrolling through social media and came across a post that felt like a gut punch. It was an acquaintance of mine—not a close friend, but someone I knew somewhat well. His post was essentially a diatribe against women. It was clearly full of anger and said things I would never have expected from this person. It was hurtful and even a bit scary. Surprising even myself, my first reaction was not anger, but panic. My mind flurried with questions about what I should do. Should I ignore it, keep scrolling, and move on with my day? This could leave the post unchanged, likely hurting many others by perpetuating feelings of misogyny and spreading misinformation about women. But the alternative—saying something—was riddled with risks. What if I said something that made him angrier or made the situation worse? What if I sounded stupid, petty, or shrill, reinforcing the negative stereotypes being conveyed?

I typed and erased and typed and erased potential responses. I wondered if any of the contacts in my phone had his number so I could reach out to him privately. (*A call from you out of the blue would not be welcome,* said my mind.) In my panic, I clearly forgot that direct messaging in social media existed. I drafted long-winded explanations (*too academic*), desperate pleas (*pathetic*), and pointed questions (*bossy*). My mind had many opinions. In the end, I took a few breaths and asked myself what it was that I wanted to accomplish. I certainly did not want to start a fight or shame the person. What I really wanted was for the post to come down, to give the person the space to take back something he clearly said in reaction to his own pain. You may have much better ideas than what I ultimately landed on, but it was all I could come up with in an attempt to accomplish my goals. I left a short comment: "Not cool, bro."

Once again, as a surprise to myself more than anyone else, this worked. With only those three words, the acquaintance edited the post to remove the hurtful content and apologized (over and beyond what I expected or hoped for!). I didn't need or ask for the apology, but my message to him spoke louder than the words it contained. It acknowledged that his post, which was born out of hurt, shouldn't have been shared publicly or directed broadly at an entire group of people. It restored my own belief in the ability for people to self-reflect and admit when they are wrong. And it restored some belief in myself as capable of confronting misogyny. I was ironically afraid of saying the wrong thing to someone who I believed had said the wrong thing, but in the end, speaking up was corrective for both of us. I think about that instance often—of the time that three simple words, on social media of all places, made a difference.

Inflexibility in Action

Now that we've defined what purposeful action is, let's discuss two ways that psychological *in*flexibility shows up: (1) inaction and (2) mindless action. Although it might seem counterintuitive, inaction *can* be purposeful (stay with us here). To paraphrase the song "Freewill" by Canadian rock band Rush, choosing *not* to decide is still making a choice. We are not necessarily endorsing 1980s rock as a vessel of wisdom, but some lyrics stand out in the cultural ethos for a reason, and this one resonated with many people. The difference between purposeful versus inflexible inaction all comes back to values. It may be psychologically flexible to disengage from a conversation, or even to avoid it in the first place, *if* you make this decision in the service of your values, such as your safety or personal mental health. Maybe you can think of a time where not talking to someone was better in the long run for both of you.

However, we often use inaction as avoidance, which involves *not* making a conscious choice at all. If Danielle had let instinctual panic guide her in the previous example, she would have closed the social media app and then tried to go about her day without dwelling on it. By now, you can guess how ineffective and likely damaging that would have been.

Can you think of a time when you wanted to take an action and didn't? What were the barriers? Were there any small actions you did take in that direction? Were there small actions you could have taken?

_____
_____
_____
_____
_____

In addition to inaction, psychological inflexibility can also show up as mindless action. As we mentioned in chapter 2, you probably know the feeling of getting to a familiar destination without much thought about the steps you took to get there. Assuming you arrive okay, this is of no real consequence. The problem arises when you engage in mindless action during activities that would otherwise be meaningful or important to you. For example, when humanitarian atrocities make you feel powerless to enact change, you may engage in "doomscrolling" or look at every social media post or news article about

Chapter 10: *Saying the Wrong Thing with Purpose*

something. Knowledge is important, and we are not suggesting that people avoid news or online dialogue. But there are certain actions that might be a better use of your time, such as volunteering or donating. However, you can only come to this realization if you use mindfulness to take a step back and acknowledge the ways in which doomscrolling is superseding important parts of your life over which you do have agency.

Can you think of a time when you acted mindlessly, zoned out, or were distracted during an important or meaningful activity? What were the barriers to remaining in the present moment during the activity? Did you recognize that this was happening in the moment, or only realize it later? Were there any actions, however small, that you did take to act more purposely in the moment?

_____
_____
_____
_____

You know as well as we do that we can't be mindful all the time, and sometimes we need mindless time to relax or recharge. Only you can determine whether inaction or mindless action is serving you and your values, or whether they are perpetuating avoidance and taking you out of your life.

The Importance of Purpose

By now, you can expect that we have some science to back us up! Yes, like the other areas of psychological flexibility, taking purposeful action is associated with a variety of positive outcomes, such as lower levels of depression (McCracken, 2013), reductions in burnout (Hess et al., 2022), and even improved physical health (McCracken, 2013)—just to name a few. And lest you think it would be too hard to improve this type of skill, purposeful action interventions improve not only the skill itself but psychological flexibility overall (Levin et al., 2020).

In contrast, when we don't intentionally act based on our values, we may find ourselves drifting aimlessly through life. You know the feeling, right? Going through routines and familiar motions, oblivious to opportunities for meaningful connection. And to be clear, we do not expect you to be 100 percent keyed into your values at every moment of every day. That would be exhausting! As with everything we have already discussed, there is always a healthy ebb and flow. Purposeful action requires that you mindfully connect to your values, assess the situation, and disentangle from the traps in your mind holding you back.

This brings us to another point: No one expects you to be perfect. We are all human and inherently flawed. So many of us have been taught that if we cannot master something quickly or be the best, then it's not worth even trying. This can creep into our decision-making and behavior patterns in all sorts of sneaky ways. Let's say you talk with your best friend about a social justice issue the two of you disagree on, and you both walk away feeling hurt and confused. It would be natural to focus on the painful outcome of this conversation and give up on taking similar opportunities in the future. On the other hand, if you were to focus on what it was like to connect with your values of honest friendship and the promotion of social justice, you might feel a little more willing to come back to the conversation with this friend at another time, perhaps having learned something from the previous interaction.

Similarly, we often believe that if we make a mistake, the whole endeavor is lost. The example of diet culture comes to mind, with concepts like "cheat days" and calorie allowances, which reinforce the idea that we must wait for a new day to start again. The beauty of purposeful action is that literally every second is a new opportunity, a new beginning! Even within a single conversation, you may realize you have lost contact with your values by raising your voice or remaining silent about something you have an opinion on. Using your mindfulness skills gives you the opportunity to take a breath, check in with why this issue matters to you, and start again.

Chapter 10: *Saying the Wrong Thing with Purpose*

> ### Monica's Story—Writing Bravely
>
> I have rarely experienced such intense avoidance and anxiety as I have while cowriting this workbook! Usually, I really enjoy writing, but I am deeply afraid of the criticism books inherently receive. I'm terrified of letting down anyone who picks up this book with high hopes and expectations. I literally worry about saying the wrong thing and causing someone anger or hurt. I am afraid of trying my best and still not being good enough. And yet, I keep coming back to this work because it aligns with my values, especially using my privilege to support individuals and communities in achieving equitable wellness and building an equitable society.
>
> When I focus on these values, I feel empowered to take braver stances in my writing and in the feedback I offer my coauthors. Happily, I've been positively reinforced for these actions by my coauthors and some of our collaborators. There are always edits and thoughtful conversations to be had, but I'm willing to keep writing bravely because it really is such a small thing in the grand scheme of life and stress and pain. So, I continue to sit down, take (many) deep breaths, dig deep, and write for you and for me.

As you can see, when you engage in purposeful action, it becomes reinforcing. Even when things don't go as planned or don't turn out in a definitively positive way, acting with purpose promotes confidence that you are doing what matters to you. That is something inherently fulfilling and nourishing.

Jess's Exercise—Hiking with Purpose

When hiking, you don't typically ascend a mountain by climbing straight uphill, which would be exhausting and potentially dangerous, but by following a series of switchback trails, which make periodic turns back and forth up the mountain to make the ascent easier and graded. Purposeful action works best with a similar approach.

This exercise will help you apply the concept of switchbacks to the goals you have in life. Think about a personal or professional goal and write it on the top of the hill. Now, think about the small steps or actions you could take to get there, and write those on each of the switchbacks. These switchbacks will make the uphill climb easier, and they'll help you make steady progress while also changing your perspective. Maybe you never get to the top of the hill, but you may encounter a scenic view by approaching one of the actions along the way with meaning and purpose.

Purposefully Working Toward Goals

As we mentioned earlier, setting goals is one component of purposeful action. If you've participated in a formal education system, you've probably been taught some goal-setting strategies. We have found that the SMART goals model works well for many of our clients (and ourselves!) when faced with a difficult task. Here's what the acronym stands for:

- **Specific:** What exactly do you want to change? Be really specific about the smallest possible action you could take.

- **Measurable:** How will you know you've met your goal? What type of data will you use to track your progress? Being able to objectively measure change makes seemingly unachievable goals attainable.

Chapter 10: *Saying the Wrong Thing with Purpose*

- **Attainable:** Speaking of, is this something you are actually able to do in your current life right now? Are there any resources needed for this goal which you lack? Do you have the time needed to take these steps? Are there any emotional, spiritual, or physical safety concerns you should address? Can you challenge yourself juuuust enough?

- **Relevant:** What value is this goal related to? How will achieving this goal impact other areas of your life? Will it alleviate a struggle or enhance something you care about? Is this aligned with who you are and want to be?

- **Time-bound:** What is your timeframe for achieving this goal? What times of day or days of the week will you be taking these actions? Is this something happening right now, or over a span of days, weeks, or months?

For example, if you value friendship and would like to take purposeful actions toward making and maintaining friends, here is what your SMART goal might look like:

- **Specific:** I would like to make three new friends.

- **Measurable:** A new friend will be defined as someone whose company I enjoy and whom I spend time with in person or over the phone once per month.

- **Achievable:** I can pursue new friendships by joining Bumble BFF or Meetups.com and by attending the weekly social run in my neighborhood. Although I don't have a car, I can walk to areas within a two-mile radius, take the city bus, or use a rideshare app. I will pursue daytime activities for now until I establish relationships I can trust.

- **Relevant:** Making more friends will help me to feel connected to a community bigger than myself. I hope it will alleviate feelings of loneliness and also fill my cup between obligations like work.

- **Time-bound:** I will accomplish this goal over the next six months, to be complete by December 1, 2025. I will try a new social avenue once weekly until the goal is achieved.

With this framework in mind, your actual goal might be to "Make three new friends (people whom I like and spend time with in person or over the phone once per month) by attending one new social event weekly. I will accomplish this by December 1, 2025." The next exercise will help you apply the concept of SMART goals to your own life.

SAYING THE *WRONG* THING

Exercise—SMART Goals

To get into the habit of setting SMART goals, think of a simple, purposeful action you'd like to take toward a value. For example, maybe you value health and your purposeful action is "improving sleep," or perhaps you value family and your purposeful action is "working on communication." No need to change the world here. Just think of a small but meaningful thing you'd like to accomplish using the SMART framework as a guide.

Value:

_____

Purposeful action in the direction of this value:

_____
_____
_____

Specific (What specific outcome do you want to accomplish?)

_____
_____
_____
_____

Measurable (What will be the evidence you've achieved it?)

_____
_____
_____
_____

Attainable (Is this doable?)

_____
_____
_____
_____

Chapter 10: *Saying the Wrong Thing with Purpose*

Relevant (How is it in service of your value?)

_____
_____
_____

Time-bound (What is your time frame for achieving this?)

_____
_____
_____

Now write a full sentence for the goal you will set, using the SMART formula. For example, if you value health and your purposeful action was to improve your sleep, your goal might be: "I will begin my bedtime routine (washing my face, brushing my teeth) at 9:30 p.m. every night and be in bed by 10:00 p.m., keeping track in my journal. I will do this for the next three months and reevaluate at that time if changes are needed."

_____
_____
_____

Having Difficult Conversations with Purpose

In chapter 1, we introduced a variety of topics that people often go to great lengths to avoid, and we underscored a common theme that underlies them all: fear and anxiety. You may think that's why we decided to title this book *Saying the Wrong Thing*. Well, the title of this book is not a fear-based exclamation, but rather a purposeful action! That's right, *Saying the Wrong Thing* is an invitation to show up fully and intentionally to important conversations, even though you might say something "wrong." Obviously, your goal is not to offend or hurt other people, but to face your fear of making a mistake rather than allowing it to hold you back. That is purposeful action.

SAYING THE *WRONG* THING

What's more, not only does purposeful action graciously allow you to "fail," but you are *expected* to. Humans learn and grow by reflecting on mistakes and exploring different ways of approaching solutions. Some may call this failure. We call it being an imperfect human in a very messy and confusing world. Committing to your values means committing to the likelihood that you will get things wrong while you figure out the most effective action for a situation. The key is to remain in contact with your values to manage the fear, anxiety, and sadness that may arise.

Mahmood's Story—To Say or Not to Say

I grew up in a "dry" or alcohol-free household and socialized with other families that similarly didn't drink. It wasn't until college that I was around social drinkers regularly. It made me very uncomfortable and uneasy, so I avoided it. In my mid-twenties, my comfort grew; I was able to tolerate being around people drinking, sometimes offering to be the designated driver for friends. It was a role I was happy to play, as allowing impaired friends to drive frightened me beyond belief. There were many times I got into arguments with friends over who was going to drive out of concern for everyone's safety. As an adult, I now have a zero-tolerance policy toward drinking and driving. Even if someone has just one drink, I insist on driving if I am not already.

But on a recent family vacation, that was not the case. My father-in-law drove the family to dinner, where he proceeded to have a couple of drinks. Every time he ordered another, I became mentally anguished. *Should I say something now? Should I say something later? What would I say? How would he react? What would I do if he reacted negatively?* As dinner progressed, my distress was palpable to my wife. Though she didn't know what I was thinking, she knew something was wrong based on my mannerisms. As a result, she became anxious and worried.

At the end of dinner, I committed to saying something by offering myself as the driver. Despite my fears, I reflected on the values behind my zero-tolerance policy. Having developed a trusting relationship with my father-in-law, I also reasoned I should trust him not to respond negatively. I approached my father-in-law while we were putting on our jackets. The first words out of his mouth were "I was going to ask you or my brother to drive." He had already been thinking to himself that he was not fit to drive. I immediately felt relief. I also judged myself as "stupid" for worrying throughout dinner about it. Had I initiated the conversation earlier, much stress would have been alleviated. Still, I felt great about his reaction and about my own willingness to approach the conversation, even if later than ideal.

Chapter 10: *Saying the Wrong Thing with Purpose*

> But not everyone felt that way. My wife later told me that my obvious distress during dinner made her anxious, leading to her not being able to enjoy herself. In a testament to her commitment and leadership despite potential discomfort, she brought the three of us together to discuss what happened. After exchanging apologies, my father-in-law made it abundantly clear that I should never worry about bringing up my concerns with him and that he will always hand over the keys should I have any concerns about alcohol consumption. While this conversation had the potential to go poorly, it instead showcased to me the importance of expressing my own needs and listening to the needs of my loved ones.

At this point, you might be thinking, *This is all well and good, but it's easier said than done.* We agree! With that in mind, here are some tips for moving toward your values and important conversations, whatever they may bring. First, remember the foundational communication skills from chapter 3:

- Practice active listening by looking for the meaning of what's being said (e.g., "reading between the lines" to see what this person cares about), asking clarifying questions, and reflecting back what you're hearing.
- Express yourself clearly by using "I" statements, practicing ahead of time, being specific, and aligning your body language with your message and tone.
- Practice empathy by imagining the other person's emotional state or putting yourself in their shoes.
- Use radical candor to provide honest and caring feedback.

These foundational skills, along with the six components of psychological flexibility, will help you feel more prepared for both planned and unexpected conversations. The key here, as always, is *practice*. Even using these skills in benign everyday conversation will make them more accessible when heavier discussions arise. We have also found the following tips and activities helpful in our own practice of purposeful action:

- **Reward yourself:** Any step you take toward showing up in difficult conversations should be rewarded! Make a list of ways you can reward yourself for using these skills. They can include indulgences like eating something delicious or buying yourself a treat, or actions like taking a peaceful walk or practicing positive affirmations.

SAYING THE *WRONG* THING

I will reward myself by:

_____

_____

_____

- **Use community for accountability:** We started offering workshops on saying the wrong thing because we realized that practicing these skills with others helped us move away from shame and guilt and toward courage. The more we talked with workshop participants and colleagues, the easier it became to remember our values and who we wanted to be in difficult conversations. If you haven't already identified a community you can share your journey with, now is the time. Write who you will go to for encouragement, for accountability, and for processing conversations that went well or poorly. This can include an online community too!

My *saying the wrong thing* community includes:

_____

_____

_____

- **Take time to reflect:** Not everyone loves journaling. But writing about your thoughts and feelings, especially in difficult situations, can help you process the experience on a deeper cognitive and emotional level. Whether you type a note on your phone, use the back pages of this book, or jot down bullet points on scrap paper, take time to reflect on missed or fulfilled opportunities. What are skills you practiced or realize now that you could have practiced? Would you do anything differently? What are you proud of yourself for, even if it didn't end well? Use mindfulness skills to reflect on what showed up in your body during and after an interaction. Make a list of reflection questions here that you want to return to after difficult conversations.

I will ask myself the following reflection questions:

_____

_____

_____

Chapter 10: *Saying the Wrong Thing with Purpose*

- **Take breaks:** It is okay to take breaks during challenging conversations so you and others can be your best selves. In fact, taking time to cool off may be necessary so you have the brain power to access your skills and values. Think about how you will know when you need a break. For example, maybe you get tunnel vision, start to see red, or have difficulty finding the words to say, or your body sends you signals of distress like sweating, rapid breathing, or a quivering voice.

I will know I need a break when:

_____
_____
_____

This is the phrase I will use to take the break I need:

_____
_____
_____

Exercise—Stand and Declare

Now that you're nearing the end of this book, it's time to take a stand and articulate your commitment for change. This will make your intentions and actions more concrete and attainable than if you just leave them rolling around in your mind.

To begin, think of a valued action you'd like to take related to a challenging conversation. For example, maybe you want to discuss a family member's voting rationale or post something meaningful, but charged, on social media. Then complete the following prompts to make this valued action a priority. After you walk through the prompts, you will stand and declare your commitment metaphorically or out loud. For the most accountability, share your commitment with a friend or community.

Start by choosing the goal you want to work toward when it comes to having difficult conversations. Reflect on what you've learned in this chapter and get specific about achieving your goal using the SMART goal framework.

_____
_____
_____

SAYING THE *WRONG* THING

Now, let's dive even deeper. What values are you moving toward with this goal? Try to reflect on why this conversation matters to you and what it would be in the service of.

_____
_____
_____

Have you been avoiding this conversation for any reason? Why hasn't it happened yet? What difficult thoughts, feelings, or sensations arise when you think about following through with your goal?

_____
_____
_____

Take a moment to breathe and mindfully reflect on your goal and the challenge it presents. What aspects of psychological flexibility might help you overcome these difficulties—either before or during the conversation? For example, will you need to practice accepting your experiences in the moment? Will you need to practice cognitive defusion to get unstuck from certain thoughts or feelings?

_____
_____
_____

Taking a compassionate stance, spend some time thinking about your own perspective and that of the other person. Are there differences in how you and the other person might perceive the situation? Do you notice if you're criticizing yourself or the other person? How might you use compassion and self-compassion to facilitate taking purposeful action?

_____
_____
_____

Okay, now it's time to stand and declare! Take the information you've reflected on above and fill in the following prompts. Then choose how you want to declare it: internally, out

Chapter 10: *Saying the Wrong Thing with Purpose*

loud, to a friend, in community, or even to your cat. Once you've declared your intention, the only thing left to do is ACT.

What I care about is: _____

_____

One thing I've been doing to avoid or control the situation is: _____

_____

I'm through with that! I'm committing to: _____

_____

Go to www.sayingthewrongthing.com/more/purpose to see what purposeful actions other readers and workshop participants are taking and to submit your own.

Play and Practice

- Keep a journal for one week, setting aside ten to thirty minutes at the end of each day to reflect and write about your day. Note what purposeful actions you took as well as any periods of inaction or mindless action.

- With a trusted person, choose some topics that are difficult to discuss. Take turns choosing topics and saying something you consider "wrong" about each one. Reflect on what feelings and thoughts come up in the moment or after, also noticing any thoughts you were not willing to say out loud. This exercise helps pull together the skills of psychological flexibility to practice *saying the wrong thing* with purpose.

- Work together with a trusted person to each come up with your own SMART goal that you want to accomplish. Declare your commitment to one another and schedule a check-in to see each other's progress. Plan a reward that you can share together once you've both completed your goal.

- Think of an important conversation you would like to have. Using the *Flexing Your Hexaflex Muscles* template at the end of this chapter, walk through all the aspects of psychological flexibility and brainstorm how you might use them to prepare for or engage in the conversation.

Takeaway Points

- Purposeful action refers to the moment-to-moment actions you take in service of what matters to you. These actions can be as small as moving your feet and as large as making meaningful change in your life or the lives of others.

- Purposeful action is not a one-time commitment that you abide by in perpetuity. You cannot succeed or fail. Sometimes, choosing not to do something or engage is equally purposeful, if it is in service of your values.

- The opposite of purposeful action is either inaction (largely driven by avoidance) or mindless action. These stop you from engaging in your life in a meaningful way.

- Purposeful action is different from, but related to, achieving goals. SMART goals are one framework for devising specific and attainable goals.

- Being purposeful and acting in accordance with your values is not always easy, and there are things you can do to help yourself along the way. Some examples include rewarding yourself and sharing your values and goals in community to enhance accountability.

Flexing Your Hexaflex Muscles

What important conversation are you hoping to have?

_____
_____
_____

What cognitive, emotional, or other barriers have been getting in the way?

_____
_____
_____

How might you use mindfulness and connect with the present moment to facilitate the conversation?

_____
_____
_____

What values are driving your desire to have this conversation that you can keep in mind as it unfolds?

_____
_____
_____

How has avoidance or control gotten in the way of having the conversation? Have there been any costs to avoiding it?

_____
_____
_____

What would it look like to approach the conversation with acceptance and willingness?
_____
_____
_____

How might you use defusion strategies and flexible perspective-taking to prepare for the conversation in advance and in the moment?
_____
_____
_____

What would it look like to approach the conversation with meaning and purpose?
_____
_____
_____

Conclusion: A Work in Progress

> "Change comes from listening, learning, caring, and conversation."
> —Gwen Ifill

Think back to the moment you found this workbook. Was it recommended to you by a friend, a coworker, or someone you trust? Did the title catch your eye because you recently worried about saying the wrong thing yourself? Were you looking for a book to recommend or gift to someone else? What values were connected to that decision? If it was recommended to you, were there shared values between you and the other person? Was there anything in your life at the time that you were actively avoiding or stuck on in some other way? Was there something you were trying to change? Finally, have you taken any actions since starting to read this book that have gotten you unstuck or moved you in the direction of what matters to you?

We hope you have learned how to treat yourself and others differently when difficult thoughts and feelings show up during important conversations. We also hope you have learned about the principles of ACT and how they can be applied in your life. Remember, you get to decide which conversations are worth showing up to. If you can step back and reflect on whether something is moving you toward your values versus control and avoidance, you will be well prepared to engage with purpose.

We started this workbook by explicitly naming our driving value of social progress. The very nature of progress means that our social contexts are always evolving, and we are no different. We are all a work in progress. As the world changes, we encourage you to continue revisiting what social progress means to you and to recognize the important conversations happening in your world at any given moment. There is cumulative power in dialogue, even between just two people, to promote change. Your values and priorities may also shift over time—we know ours have, even since we first started working on this project!—so we invite you to remain flexible with yourself as you evolve.

SAYING THE *WRONG* THING

This workbook is intended to be used again and again for building conversational skills and engaging in meaningful activities as you continue to stretch and grow over time. For this reason, we've included blank templates of all the exercises, as well as additional resources and opportunities to engage in this work, on our website: www.sayingthewrongthing.com.

You now have all the tools you need to engage in important conversations with intention and compassion. Our hope for you (and if we're being honest, for ourselves) is that you can find courage and authenticity in the power of your own voice. Be brave and take heart in the reverberations that even your messiest contributions will have on your community. Change is noble work and worth fighting for—even when that pesky fear of saying the wrong thing threatens to stand in your way.

Bibliography

Abramson, L., Uzefovsky, F., Toccaceli, V., & Knafo-Noam, A. (2020). The genetic and environmental origins of emotional and cognitive empathy: Review and meta-analyses of twin studies. *Neuroscience & Biobehavioral Reviews, 114*, 113–133. https://doi.org/10.1016/j.neubiorev.2020.03.023

Akbari, M., Seydavi, M., Hosseini, Z. S., Krafft, J., & Levin, M. E. (2022). Experiential avoidance in depression, anxiety, obsessive-compulsive related, and posttraumatic stress disorders: A comprehensive systematic review and meta-analysis. *Journal of Contextual Behavioral Science, 24*, 65–78. https://doi.org/10.1016/j.jcbs.2022.03.007

Baranoff, J., Hanrahan, S. J., & Connor, J. P. (2015). The roles of acceptance and catastrophizing in rehabilitation following anterior cruciate ligament reconstruction. *Journal of Science and Medicine in Sport, 18*(3), 250–254. https://doi.org/10.1016/j.jsams.2014.04.002

Bradley, W. J., Bodalski, E. A., de Arellano, A., Looby, A., Taylor, S. G., Canu, W., Serrano, J. W., & Flory, K. (2024). The relation between ADHD symptoms and alcohol and cannabis use outcomes in a cross-sectional study of college students: The mediating role of experiential avoidance. *Journal of Contextual Behavioral Science, 31*, Article 100727. https://doi.org/10.1016/j.jcbs.2024.100727

Breines, J. G., & Chen, S. (2012). Self-compassion increases self-improvement motivation. *Personality and Social Psychology Bulletin, 38*(9), 1133–1143. https://doi.org/10.1177/0146167212445599

Britt, T. W., Crane, M., Hodson, S. E., & Adler, A. B. (2016). Effective and ineffective coping strategies in a low-autonomy work environment. *Journal of Occupational Health Psychology, 21*(2), 154–168. https://doi.org/10.1037/a0039898

Ceary, C. D., Donahue, J. J., & Shaffer, K. (2019). The strength of pursuing your values: Valued living as a path to resilience among college students. *Stress and Health, 35*(4), 532–541. https://doi.org/10.1002/smi.2886

Cheang, R., Gillions, A., & Sparkes, E. (2019). Do mindfulness-based interventions increase empathy and compassion in children and adolescents: A systematic review. *Journal of Child and Family Studies, 28*, 1765–1779. https://doi.org/10.1007/s10826-019-01413-9

Cherry, K. M., Vander Hoeven, E., Patterson, T. S., & Lumley, M. N. (2021). Defining and measuring "psychological flexibility": A narrative scoping review of diverse flexibility and rigidity constructs and perspectives. *Clinical Psychology Review, 84*, Article 101973. https://doi.org/10.1016/j.cpr.2021.101973

Ciarrochi, J., Kashdan, T. B., Leeson, P., Heaven, P., & Jordan, C. (2011). On being aware and accepting: A one-year longitudinal study into adolescent well-being. *Journal of Adolescence, 34*(4), 695–703. https://doi.org/10.1016/j.adolescence.2010.09.003

Colle, L., Dimaggio, G., Carcione, A., Nicolò, G., Semerari, A., & Chiavarino, C. (2020). Do competitive contexts affect mindreading performance? *Frontiers in Psychology, 11*, Article 1284. https://doi.org/10.3389/fpsyg.2020.01284

Cuff, B. M. P., Brown, S. J., Taylor, L., & Howat, D. J. (2016). Empathy: A review of the concept. *Emotion Review, 8*(2), 144–153. https://doi.org/10.1177/1754073914558466

Dass, R. (1978). *Be here now, remember*. Hunuman Foundation.

Davis, E. L., Deane, F. P., & Lyons, G. C. (2015). Acceptance and valued living as critical appraisal and coping strengths for caregivers dealing with terminal illness and bereavement. *Palliative & Supportive Care, 13*(2), 359–368. https://doi.org/10.1017/S1478951514000431

Davis, M. (2024). *The becoming boundaried bootcamp*. https://boundaried.com/bootcamp

Drollinger, T., Comer, L. B., & Warrington, P. T. (2006). Development and validation of the active empathetic listening scale. *Psychology & Marketing, 23*(2), 161–180. https://doi.org/10.1002/mar.20105

Dunn, T. J., & Dimolareva, M. (2022). The effect of mindfulness-based interventions on immunity-related biomarkers: A comprehensive meta-analysis of randomised controlled trials. *Clinical Psychology Review, 92*, Article 102124. https://doi.org/10.1016/j.cpr.2022.102124

Dvorak, R. D., Sargent, E. M., Kilwein, T. M., Stevenson, B. L., Kuvaas, N. J., & Williams, T. J. (2014). Alcohol use and alcohol-related consequences: Associations with emotion regulation difficulties. *The American Journal of Drug and Alcohol Abuse, 40*(2), 125–130. https://doi.org/10.3109/00952990.2013.877920

Espel, H. M., Goldstein, S. P., Manasse, S. M., & Juarascio, A. S. (2016). Experiential acceptance, motivation for recovery, and treatment outcome in eating disorders. *Eating and Weight Disorders, 21*, 205–210. https://doi.org/10.1007/s40519-015-0235-7

Fassaert, T., van Dulmen, S., Schellevis, F., & Bensing, J. (2007). Active listening in medical consultations: Development of the Active Listening Observation Scale (ALOS-global). *Patient Education and Counseling, 68*(3), 258–264. https://doi.org/10.1016/j.pec.2007.06.011

Fields, J. S., Browne, R. K., Wieman, S. T., Lord, K. A., Orsillo, S. M., & Liverant, G. I. (2022). Associations between valued living and responsiveness to daily rewards. *Journal of Contextual Behavioral Science, 26*, 193–200. https://doi.org/10.1016/j.jcbs.2022.10.005

Fonseca, A., Monteiro, F., & Canavarro, M. C. (2018). Dysfunctional beliefs towards motherhood and postpartum depressive and anxiety symptoms: Uncovering the role of experiential avoidance. *Journal of Clinical Psychology, 74*(12), 2134–2144. https://doi.org/10.1002/jclp.22649

Gagnon, J., Dionne, F., & Pychyl, T. A. (2016). Committed action: An initial study on its association to procrastination in academic settings. *Journal of Contextual Behavioral Sciences, 5*(2), 97–102. https://doi.org/10.1016/j.jcbs.2016.04.002

Galán, S., Roy, R., Solé, E., Racine, M., de la Vega, R., Jensen, M. P., & Miró, J. (2019). Committed action, disability and perceived health in individuals with fibromyalgia. *Behavioral Medicine, 45*(1), 62–69. https://doi.org/10.1080/08964289.2018.1467370

Garey, L., Farris, S. G., Schmidt, N. B., & Zvolensky, M. J. (2016). The role of smoking-specific experiential avoidance in the relation between perceived stress and tobacco dependence, perceived barriers to cessation, and problems during quit attempts among treatment-seeking smokers. *Journal of Contextual Behavioral Science, 5*(1), 58–63. https://doi.org/10.1016/j.jcbs.2015.11.001

Gerhart, J. I., Baker, C. N., Hoerger, M., & Ronan, G. F. (2014). Experiential avoidance and interpersonal problems: A moderated mediation model. *Journal of Contextual Behavioral Science, 3*(4), 291–298. https://doi.org/10.1016/j.jcbs.2014.08.003

Gilbert, P. (2017). Compassion: Definitions and controversies. In P. Gilbert (Ed.), *Compassion: Concepts, research and applications* (pp. 3–15). Routledge.

Gilbert, P., Basran, J., MacArthur, M., Kirby, J. N. (2019). Differences in the semantics of prosocial words: an exploration of compassion and kindness. *Mindfulness, 10*, 2259–2271. https://doi.org/10.1007/s12671-019-01191-x

Godbee, M., & Kangas, M. (2022). Focusing on the self in context as an emotion regulatory strategy: An evaluation of the "self-as-context" component of ACT compared to cognitive reappraisal in managing stress. *Anxiety, Stress, & Coping, 35*(5), 557–573. https://doi.org/10.1080/10615806.2021.1985472

Graham, J. R., West, L., & Roemer, L. (2015). A preliminary exploration of the moderating role of valued living in the relationships between racist experiences and anxious and depressive symptoms. *Journal of Contextual Behavioral Science, 4*(1), 48–55. https://doi.org/10.1016/j.jcbs.2014.11.001

Bibliography

Hayes, S. C., Luoma, J. B., Bond, F. W., Masuda, A., & Lillis, J. (2006). Acceptance and commitment therapy: Model, processes and outcomes. *Behaviour research and therapy*, *44*(1), 1–25. https://doi.org/10.1016/j.brat.2005.06.006

Hess, A., Garcia, Y., Gould, E., Catagnus, R. (2022). Enhancing supervisory relationships with values and committed action training. *Journal of Contextual Behavioral Science, 26*, 241–252. https://doi.org/10.1016/j.jcbs.2022.10.009

Hoge, E. A., Acabchuk, R. L., Kimmel, H., Moitra, E., Britton, W. B., Dumais, T., Ferrer, R. A., Lazar, S. W., Vago, D., Lipsky, J., Schuman-Olivier, Z., Cheaito, A., Sager, L., Peters, S., Rahrig, H., Acero, P., Scharf, J., Loucks, E. B., & Fulwiler, C. (2021). Emotion-related constructs engaged by mindfulness-based interventions: A systematic review and meta-analysis. *Mindfulness*, *12*, 1041–1062. tps://doi.org/10.1007/s12671-020-01561-w

Howarth, A., Smith, J. G., Perkins-Porras, L., & Ussher, M. (2019). Effects of brief mindfulness-based interventions on health-related outcomes: A systematic review. *Mindfulness, 10*(10), 1957–1968. https://doi.org/10.1007/s12671-019-01163-1

Jung, W. H., & Kim, N. H. (2020). Hippocampal functional connectivity mediates the impact of acceptance on posttraumatic stress symptom severity. *Frontiers in Psychiatry, 11*, Article 753. https://doi.org/10.3389/fpsyt.2020.00753

Kabat-Zinn, J. (2003). Mindfulness-based interventions in context: Past, present, and future. *Clinical Psychology Science and Practice, 10*(2), 144–156. https://doi.org/10.1093/clipsy.bpg016

Kawamichi, H., Yoshihara, K., Sasaki, A. T., Sugawara, S. K., Tanabe, H. C., Shinohara, R., Sugisawa, Y., Tokutake, K., Mochizuki, Y., Anme, T., & Sadato, N. (2015). Perceiving active listening activates the reward system and improves the impression of relevant experiences. *Social Neuroscience, 10*(1), 16–26. https://doi.org/10.1080/17470919.2014.954732

Khoury, B., Lecomte, T., Fortin, G., Masse, M., Therien, P., Bouchard, V., Chapleau, M., Paquin, K., & Hofmann, S. G. (2013). Mindfulness-based therapy: A comprehensive meta-analysis. *Clinical Psychology Review, 33*(6), 763–771. https://doi.org/10.1016/j.cpr.2013.05.005

Klimecki, O. M., & Singer, T. (2017). The compassionate brain. In E. M. Seppälä, E. Simon-Thomas, S. L. Brown, M. C. Worline, C. D. Cameron, & J. R. Doty (Eds.), *The Oxford handbook of compassion science* (pp. 109–120). Oxford University Press.

Kübler-Ross, E. (1997). *On death and dying*. Scribner.

Larsson, A., Hooper, N., Osborne, L. A., Bennett, P., & McHugh, L. (2016). Using brief cognitive restructuring and cognitive defusion techniques to cope with negative thoughts. *Behavior Modification, 40*(3), 452–482. https://doi.org/10.1177/0145445515621488

Leary, M. R., Tate, E. B., Adams, C. E., Batts Allen, A., & Hancock, J. (2007). Self-compassion and reactions to unpleasant self-relevant events: The implications of treating oneself kindly. *Journal of Personality and Social Psychology, 92*(5), 887–904. https://doi.org/10.1037/0022-3514.92.5.887

Levin, M. E., Haeger, J., An, W., & Twohig, M. P. (2018). Comparing cognitive defusion and cognitive restructuring delivered through a mobile app for individuals high in self-criticism. *Cognitive Therapy and Research, 42*, 844–855. https://doi.org/10.1007/s10608-018-9944-3

Levin, M. E., Krafft, J., Hicks, E. T., Pierce, B., Twohig, B. T. (2020). A randomized dismantling trial of the open and engaged components of acceptance and commitment therapy in an online intervention for distressed college students. *Behaviour Research and Therapy, 126*, Article 103557. https://doi.org/10.1016/j.brat.2020.103557

Linehan, M. M. (2014). *DBT skills training handouts and worksheets* (2nd ed.). Guilford Press.

Maitland, D. W. (2020). Experiential avoidance and fear of intimacy: A contextual behavioral account of loneliness and resulting psychopathology symptoms. *Journal of Contextual Behavioral Science, 18*, 193–200. https://doi.org/10.1016/j.jcbs.2020.10.002

Marcinkiewicz, A. (2020). *Evaluating committed actions during acceptance and commitment training for caregivers of people with neurodevelopmental disabilities* [Unpublished Master's Thesis]. Brock University. https://brocku.scholaris.ca/items/61bee08e-c55b-4851-8d7a-dddec96a6eed

Martin, A. F., Walker, S. P., & Mchugh, L. A. (2023). Perspective taking as a predictor of burnout among competitive adolescent squash players. *South African Journal for Research in Sport, Physical Education and Recreation, 45*(2), 63–80. https://doi.org/10.36386/sajrsper.v45i2.180

Masuda, A., Hayes, S. C., Sackett, C. F., & Twohig, M. P. (2004). Cognitive defusion and self-relevant negative thoughts: Examining the impact of a ninety year old technique. *Behaviour Research and Therapy, 42*(4), 477–485. https://doi.org/10.1016/j.brat.2003.10.008

Mental Health America. (2021). *The state of mental health in America: 2021 online report.* https://mhanational.org/sites/default/files/2021%20State%20of%20Mental%20Health%20in%20America_0.pdf

McCracken, L. M. (2013). Committed action: An application of the psychological flexibility model to activity patterns in chronic pain. *The Journal of Pain, 14* (8), 828–835. https://doi.org/10.1016/j.jpain.2013.02.009

McNaughton, D., Hamlin, D., McCarthy, J., Head-Reeves, D., & Schreiner, M. (2008). Learning to listen: Teaching an active listening strategy to preservice education professionals. *Topics in Early Childhood Special Education, 27*(4), 223–231. https://doi.org/10.1177/0271121407311241

Mharapara, T. L., & Staniland, N. A. (2020). Radical candor: Creating a feedback culture based on learner care and empowerment. *Industrial and Organizational Psychology, 13*(4), 536–539. https://doi.org/10.1017/iop.2020.94

Mineyama, S., Tsutsumi, A., Takao, S., Nishiuchi, K., & Kawakami, N. (2007). Supervisors' attitudes and skills for active listening with regard to working conditions and psychological stress reactions among subordinate workers. *Journal of Occupational Health, 49*(2), 81–87. https://doi.org/10.1539/joh.49.81

Moran, O., Almada, P., & McHugh, L. (2018). An investigation into the relationship between the three selves (self-as-content, self-as-process and self-as-context) and mental health in adolescents. *Journal of Contextual Behavioral Science, 7*, 55–62. https://doi.org/10.1016/j.jcbs.2018.01.002

Morton, M. L., Helminen, E. C., & Felver, J. C. (2020). A systematic review of mindfulness interventions on psychophysiological responses to acute stress. *Mindfulness, 11*, 2039–2054. https://doi.org/10.1007/s12671-020-01386-7

Moscardini, E. H., Breaux, E. A., Oakey-Frost, D. N., & Tucker, R. P. (2024). Examining aspects of psychological flexibility within the integrated motivational-volitional model of suicidal behavior: A prospective investigation. *Suicide and Life-Threatening Behavior, 54*(3), 425–436. https://doi.org/10.1111/sltb.13059

Nakamura, Y. M., & Orth, U. (2005). Acceptance as a coping reaction: Adaptive or not? *Swiss Journal of Psychology, 64*(4), 281–292. https://doi.org/10.1024/1421-0185.64.4.281

Neff, K. D. (2003). The development and validation of a scale to measure self-compassion. *Self and Identity, 2*(3), 223–250. https://doi.org/10.1080/15298860309027

Neff, K. D., Rude, S. S., & K. L. Kirkpatrick. (2007). An examination of self-compassion in relation to positive psychological functioning and personality traits. *Journal of Research in Personality, 41*, 908–916. https://doi.org/10.1016/j.jrp.2006.08.002

Pakenham, K. I., Landi, G., Cattivelli, R., Grandi, S., & Tossani, E. (2023). Identification of psychological flexibility and inflexibility profiles during the COVID-19 pandemic. *Journal of Clinical Psychology, 79*(10), 2225–2250. https://doi.org/10.1002/jclp.23536

Pavlacic, J. M., Schulenberg, S. E., & Buchanan, E. M. (2021). Experiential avoidance and meaning in life as predictors of valued living: A daily diary study. *Journal of Prevention and Health Promotion, 2*(1), 135–159. https://doi.org/10.1177/2632077021998261

Rogers, C. R., & Farson, R. E. (1957). *Active listening.* The University of Chicago.

Bibliography

Şahin, O., Nalbant, A., & Yavuz, K. F. (2022). Predictors of social functioning in people with antisocial personality disorder. *Journal of Psychiatry and Neurological Sciences, 35*(2), 93–100. http://doi.org/10.14744/DAJPNS.2022.00180

Salehinejad, M. A., Ghanavati, E., Rashid, M. H. A., & Nitsche, M. A. (2021). Hot and cold executive functions in the brain: A prefrontal-cingular network. *Brain and Neuroscience Advances, 5*, 1–19. https://doi.org/10.1177/23982128211007769

Sauer, S. E., & Baer, R. A. (2009). Responding to negative internal experience: Relationships between acceptance and change-based approaches and psychological adjustment. *Journal of Psychopathology and Behavioral Assessment, 31*, 378–386. https://doi.org/10.1007/s10862-009-9127-3

Scott, K. (2017). Understand what motivates each person on your team. *Leader to Leader, 2017*(86), 34–40. https://doi.org/10.1002/ltl.20319

Scott, K. (2019). *Radical candor: Fully revised & updated edition: Be a kick-ass boss without losing your humanity*. St. Martin's Press.

Selič-Zupančič, P., Klemenc-Ketiš, Z., & Onuk Tement, S. (2023). The impact of psychological interventions with elements of mindfulness on burnout and well-being in healthcare professionals: A systematic review. *Journal of Multidisciplinary Healthcare, 16*, 1821–1831. https://doi.org/10.2147/JMDH.S398552

Suarez, J. L. (2021). *Are dementia caregivers planning for their own future? A needs assessment and examination of barriers to services* [Unpublished master's thesis]. State University of New York at New Paltz.

Tan, J. S. T. (2022). Hiding behind the "perfect" mask: A phenomenological study of Filipino university students' lived experiences of perfectionism. *International Journal of Qualitative Studies on Health and Well-Being, 17*(1), Article 2062819. https://doi.org/10.1080/17482631.2022.2062819

Thompson, E. M., Brierley, M. E. E., Destrée, L., Albertella, L., & Fontenelle, L. F. (2022). Psychological flexibility and inflexibility in obsessive-compulsive symptom dimensions, disability, and quality of life: An online longitudinal study. *Journal of Contextual Behavioral Science, 23*, 38–47. https://doi.org/10.1016/j.jcbs.2021.11.004

Tunç, H., Morris, P. G., Kyranides, M. N., McArdle, A., McConachie, D., & Williams, J. (2023). The relationships between valued living and depression and anxiety: A systematic review, meta-analysis, and meta-regression. *Journal of Contextual Behavioral Science, 28*, 102–126. https://doi.org/10.1016/j.jcbs.2023.02.004

Tyndall, I., Waldeck, D., Riva, P., Wesselmann, E. D., & Pancani, L. (2018). Psychological flexibility and ostracism: Experiential avoidance rather than cognitive fusion moderates distress from perceived ostracism over time. *Journal of Contextual Behavioral Science, 7*, 72–80. https://doi.org/10.1016/j.jcbs.2018.02.001

Verhaeghen, P. (2021). Mindfulness as attention training: Meta-analyses on the links between attention performance and mindfulness interventions, long-term meditation practice, and trait mindfulness. *Mindfulness, 12*, 564–581. https://doi.org/10.1007/s12671-020-01532-1

Wegner, D. M., Schneider, D. J., Carter, S. R., & White, T. L. (1987). Paradoxical effects of thought suppression. *Journal of Personality and Social Psychology, 53*(1), 5–13. https://doi.org/10.1037/0022-3514.53.1.5

Weisz, E., & Cikara, M. (2021). Strategic regulation of empathy. *Trends in Cognitive Sciences, 25*(3), 213–227. https://doi.org/10.1016/j.tics.2020.12.002

Wiech, K., & Tracey, I. (2009). The influence of negative emotions on pain: Behavioral effects and neural mechanisms. *Neuroimage, 47*(3), 987–994. https://doi.org/10.1016/j.neuroimage.2009.05.059

Winter, F., Steffan, A., Warth, M., Ditzen, B., & Aguilar-Raab, C. (2021). Mindfulness-based couple interventions: A systematic literature review. *Family Process, 60*(3), 694–711. https://doi.org/10.1111/famp.12683

Winter, R., Issa, E., Roberts, N., Norman, R. I., & Howick, J. (2020). Assessing the effect of empathy-enhancing interventions in health education and training: a systematic review of randomised controlled trials. *BMJ Open, 10*(9), Article e036471. https://doi.org/10.1136/bmjopen-2019-036471

Yu, L., Norton, S., & McCracken, L. M. (2017). Change in "self-as-context" ("perspective-taking") occurs in acceptance and commitment therapy for people with chronic pain and is associated with improved functioning. *The Journal of Pain, 18*(6), 664–672. https://doi.org/10.1016/j.jpain.2017.01.005

Acknowledgments

We want to thank the PESI Publishing team, especially Kayla for guiding us and Jenessa for finding and enhancing the singular thread through her editing. Thank you to our contributors for sharing your stories, expertise, and vulnerability to make the content deeper and richer than we could ever have done alone. We are grateful to Erica, Stephanie, and Christie for their preliminary reviews and encouraging feedback. Many thanks to Ted Tucker for his kind assistance and expertise in recording and editing our mindfulness audio tracks. Thanks to Dr. Amy Murrell for her mentorship and guidance in our early ACT training.

Thank you to all the friends who have enthusiastically encouraged and reminded us of the timeliness of this endeavor. We each have been invaluably influenced by the vulnerabilities and trust of our clients, colleagues, students, and loved ones, who have taught us what it means to be brave and to rebound from saying the wrong thing. We hope our work here honors your openness and contributes to a world in which you feel safe and valued.

Danielle: I would like to thank Drs. Emily Sandoz and Matthieu Villatte for not only introducing me to ACT but also making sure I understood and appreciated the underlying science. To my parents, Mel and Dan, I am forever grateful for the confidence and daring that you instilled in me. To my sister, Christie, you have always been both an inspiration and one of my greatest supporters. Your influence, and especially your humor, can be found throughout these pages. And above all, I want to thank my partner, Brian. Thank you for grounding me when anxiety threatens to carry me away, for being an absolutely endless source of knowledge, and for supporting ideas that would otherwise seem wildly unrealistic without your firm belief in my ability to make them a reality.

Monica: I have to start with gratitude toward my husband. Chad, I am endlessly thankful for your limitless support, insight, and grounding. Thank you for always believing in me and being my steadfast tree. To my parents (Dan and Terri) and my sisters (Laura, Stephanie, and Rachael): I know I say a lot of "wrong" things when I'm impassioned. Thanks for loving and seeing me, and for always finding ways of moving forward together. To my APDC family: Thank you for allowing me to find a home with you, and thank you for all your patience and love throughout my growing pains.

SAYING THE *WRONG* THING

Molly: I would like to thank my parents, Karen and Tommy, and siblings (Savanna, Tommy, Lyla, and Gentry) for their vibrant souls and unconditional love. As the middle child, navigating difficult conversations was a huge part of the curriculum. Though I've often said the wrong thing, my status has never diminished in your eyes; I'm so grateful for that. To my darling husband, Charlie, and sweet baby, Jules: You are the lovelights that illuminate all that matters and extinguish all that does not. I never knew I could be so happy. I love you, I love you, I love you.

About the Authors

DANIELLE N. MOYER, PhD (she/her) is an associate professor in the Department of Pediatrics at Oregon Health & Science University within the divisions of psychology and endocrinology. She is a licensed psychologist in the state of Oregon and the director of psychology for the OHSU Doernbecher Gender Clinic, which serves the medical, social, and mental health needs of transgender and gender-diverse youth and their families. Danielle also specializes  in mindfulness and acceptance-based interventions for youth and families. Her work involves clinical service, individual and systemic advocacy, training and education, consultation to medical and mental health providers, and clinical research. In her spare time, Danielle enjoys lounging around with her husband and cat, reading a good fantasy novel, and tapping into her creative side. She is proud to say she has a particular talent for writing song parodies.

MONICA M. GERBER, PhD (she/her) is a licensed clinical psychologist at the Asian Pacific Clinic of Aurora Mental Health and Recovery in Colorado. She specializes in providing culturally and trauma-informed care to individuals and families with refugee and immigrant experiences. She trains and supports graduate students to enter the mental health field with anti-oppressive and community-driven orientations in her role guiding clinical training  at the Cultural Development and Wellness Center. Monica has worked in community settings throughout her career and incorporates an understanding of systemic oppression and community healing into her clinical work, teaching, and supervision. She is a sixth-generation American of primarily German and English heritage and lives with a visual deficit. Monica enjoys eating long meals with friends, reading a good book, and being nourished by the natural world with her husband and two elderly fur babies.

SAYING THE *WRONG* THING

MOLLY S. TUCKER, PhD (she/her) is a clinical psychologist residing in Tucson, Arizona, and licensed in the state of California, where she sees clients virtually. She works in private practice and specializes in serving adult individuals who are seeking clarity about their purpose, innate creativity, life balance, and boundaries. Molly also works with couples to promote deeper and more authentic connections by balancing respectful and honest communication. She utilizes mindfulness, compassion, and attachment-based approaches and is committed to cultivating a nonjudgmental space where all can feel accepted and dignified. Molly finds peace and perspective in nature, spending ample time hiking, visiting national parks, and traveling to witness this beautiful world. She is a new mother and most enjoys spending her days reveling in childlike wonder of being alive with her son and husband. Molly adores the Beatles and aspires to the lifestyle of hobbits.

Notes